# ROUTLEDGE LIBRARY EDITIONS: EDUCATION

# COMPARATIVE STUDIES AND EDUCATIONAL DECISION

# COMPARATIVE STUDIES AND EDUCATIONAL DECISION

EDMUND J. KING

Volume 7

LONDON AND NEW YORK

First published in 1968

This edition first published in 2012
by Routledge
2 Park Square, Milton Park, Abingdon, Oxfordshire OX14 4RN

Simultaneously published in the USA and Canada
by Routledge
711 Third Avenue, New York, NY 10017

First issued in paperback 2014

*Routledge is an imprint of the Taylor & Francis Group, an informa business*

© 1968 The Bobbs-Merrill Company, Inc.

All rights reserved. No part of this book may be reprinted or reproduced or utilised in any form or by any electronic, mechanical, or other means, now known or hereafter invented, including photocopying and recording, or in any information storage or retrieval system, without permission in writing from the publishers.

*Trademark notice*: Product or corporate names may be trademarks or registered trademarks, and are used only for identification and explanation without intent to infringe.

*British Library Cataloguing in Publication Data*
A catalogue record for this book is available from the British Library

ISBN 13: 978-0-415-66834-7 (Volume 7)
ISBN 13: 978-1-138-00838-0 (pbk)

**Publisher's Note**
The publisher has gone to great lengths to ensure the quality of this reprint but points out that some imperfections in the original copies may be apparent.

**Disclaimer**
The publisher has made every effort to trace copyright holders and would welcome correspondence from those they have been unable to trace.

*Edmund J. King*

# COMPARATIVE STUDIES AND EDUCATIONAL DECISION

*Methuen Educational Ltd.*
*11 New Fetter Lane London EC4*

*First published in Great Britain in 1968 by*
*Methuen Educational Ltd.*
*11 New Fetter Lane London EC4*
*Copyright © 1968 by The Bobbs-Merrill Company, Inc.*
*Printed in the United States of America*

## preface

Books about education, already plentiful, become more numerous every week. Why add another? One obvious answer is that few manufactures date as fast as books about education. The world is already in full change, and is using education for unprecedented purposes on an ever larger scale and with growing impatience. The content, context, and commitment of education are without precedent. Keeping up with change at home is more than a full-time job, and when we look abroad the changes appear more cataclysmic still.

That truism is at least a justification for books on comparative education. What are other people doing? What problems, aims, and methods are relevant to us? Does such a study help our decisions? Of course; and the growing popularity of books on comparative education is proof enough. Articles in this field are finding their way into popular journals, and into the scientific periodicals of other disciplines, as well as into business journals. All this would have been unthinkable a generation or two ago; yet the great interest already shown looks like being only the outer ripple of a huge tide of mounting concern. The questions are not only about what other people do, or why; they are more than ever directed towards the question, "What can we do about it ourselves?"

Books on comparative education are seldom slanted towards that question. The few that have some bearing on it usually concentrate on pedagogical aspects of peculiar interest to teachers (or indeed only to future teachers with an examination to pass). The results in some cases are disastrous—for the books themselves, for comparative education generally, and for public decision. On the other hand, there have been outstandingly good contributions to comparative education. More continue to be made, not always by scholars ostensibly in this particular field. At the present stage of educational development and decision it seems important to take stock of overall direction and possibilities in our field, and above all to assess our relevance to others' decisions in education.

Some helpful observations have been made by respected colleagues in comparative education, whose works are referred to in the text. Why then another book from me? An article of mine on methodology and purpose appeared in the *Comparative Education Review* (New York, June, 1959); and a more recent essay on "The purpose of comparative education," in *Comparative Education* (Oxford, June, 1965), has been very widely distributed as an offprint. Furthermore, each book in the *Society, Schools and Progress* series of comparative surveys of particular countries contains an introduction by myself which relates comparative studies of education to the present vogue of comparative studies in other academic disciplines. In some ways that would seem enough, when added to the methodological and theoretical surveys offered elsewhere, especially in view of my own reluctance to theorise and speculate when so much hard study and planning remains to be done.

On the other hand, from Vancouver to Tokyo I have been asked for advice or talks on methodology, or "a conceptual framework" for comparative education today. Would-be colleagues in many countries are evidently at a loss. They are perplexed about the future development of comparative education itself. They wonder how best to introduce it to their own students. They are uncertain about its relationship to other academic disciplines or to the world of practical decisions. Scholars of repute working in areas adjacent to comparative education are sometimes more uncertain still.

What finally decided me (though I had long felt an obligation to do something in the present debate on purpose and method) was the announcement by a Japanese firm of publishers that they intended to produce a Japanese translation of my "book" on purpose and method in comparative education. (The reference was to my 1965 article.) At about the same time there was an enquiry from another overseas publisher. Therefore I felt obliged to set some ideas on paper in book form—ideas found helpful in many countries in discussion with colleagues and advanced students. They are here addressed partly to such people, but also to colleagues and friends beyond the strict confines of my own discipline. I refer to those whose primary interests may be in the field of the theory of knowledge or else in its very practical counterpart, political or administrative decision. In any case I feel that academic, practical and civic concerns are complementary interests these days.

It goes without saying that the present book is far from being a final statement by myself, let alone others. It is an interim thesis only. But I shall be more than content if this statement of my own ideas, and of others' reactions and insights which I have absorbed, helps further discussion of comparative studies.

EDMUND KING

LONDON, 1967

## contents

LIST OF FIGURES … x

*one*    IS THERE A SCIENCE OF EDUCATIONAL PREDICTION? … 1

*two*    IS OUR STUDY OF EDUCATION OBJECTIVE? … 23

*three*    COMPARATIVE EDUCATION: A METHOD OF ANALYSIS AND ENQUIRY … 43

*four*    COMMITMENT AND STRATEGY IN COMPARATIVE EDUCATION … 71

*five*    THE STRUCTURE OF INFORMED DECISION … 103

*six*    A PROGRESSION OF COMPARATIVE STUDY … 137

SELECTED BIBLIOGRAPHY … 167

INDEX … 175

## list of figures

1. The supposed relationship of a "detached" observer regarding an object ... 26
2. The relationship between an observer and an object observed on a particular occasion ... 27
3. The part played by roles in influencing personal perception or decision ... 29
4. The "personality" or preoccupations of a school system ... 31
5. The aspects of "science" in relation to social or political decision ... 38
6. Flow diagram illustrating possible factors in educational decision and growth ... 112
7. Continuing structure of decision, implementation, and review ... 123

*one*

# IS THERE A SCIENCE OF EDUCATIONAL PREDICTION?

Why comparative studies? All around us we see university departments of comparative law, comparative religion, comparative physiology and anatomy, while commerce and scientific research for their part constantly make comparisons between domestic production or activities and those of other countries. One major field of comparison is in the study of education. But it is impossible to divorce educational trends and needs from comparative studies of society, economics, and technology undergoing rapid change—all with a view to prediction and decision. It will be a major purpose of this book to show why such a divorce is unthinkable,[1] and why a study of

---

[1] Some detailed examples, related to more practical matters of educational policy and reform, are to be found in my *Education and Social Change* (Oxford: Pergamon Press 1966).

the evidence which can be brought in from other academic disciplines and fields of experience can help the more scientific penetration of the problems of education itself. Yet, without waiting for this theoretical justification, we can see all around us a growing concern for effectiveness (indeed, relevance) in education. Decisions must be reliable producers of results. These qualities are publicly and privately assessed by judgements or studies comparatively made by governments, commercial houses, industries, and anxious parents, no less than by the academic community itself. That is not surprising when education is already the biggest single item (after defence) in many national budgets, and is in any case relied on as the principal means of shaping the future so as to produce a better world and a more constructive prospect for mankind.

Comparative studies in relation to education are not new; they have been undertaken for at least two thousand years. During the past century and a half they have achieved international prominence and have produced some outstandingly good work. However, the changes which have overtaken education itself—and, more pertinently, have overtaken the study of society in full change—have brought comparative studies to a new degree of urgency. That is partly because so much is at stake. It is also because we recognise that so much more can be achieved by systematic preparation and study. The very prolificacy of comparative study and research, and the still more generous flow of writing on this theme, have made it necessary to undertake a comprehensive review of present achievements and prospects. If that is not done, unco-ordinated activities and sectional interests each claim a kind of orthodoxy of their own, like so many warring sects, while overlooking the very need for which comparative studies have always been undertaken—the need for an overall awareness to be built of constituent items of information and regularised by complementary methods of analysis together with co-ordinated plans for the future.

Much confusion reigns at present. In consequence, much comparative study relevant to education is confined within the increasingly segregated walls of some teachers' colleges. Governments and commercial or industrial enterprises now conduct their own comparisons of attainments, techniques, and objectives. National research units, sometimes connected with formal education and sometimes with strategic or commercial interests, undertake comparative analyses and predictions, while international agencies also make large regional or special-interest surveys of a comparative kind. The comparisons and analyses are certainly needed; but can they be effective if they ignore unsuspected educational and cultural factors affecting their predictions?

The grave risk is that all this enterprise may thrive and produce important educational and political decisions likely to have far-reaching effects—but without benefit of the information, techniques, and subtler insights of the academic students of education in universities and colleges. This relatively neglected band, furthermore, may themselves lose touch with what really matters in comparative studies to-day, when education has ceased to be a matter of theory or speculation related to a small minority but is at the very centre of all public decisions of any significance whatsoever. To say as much as this is not simply to cry, "Wolf". Neither is it a Jeremiad against the activities of those undertaking comparative study and analyses in places outside the universities and colleges. It is, rather, a recognition of the great importance and *interdependence* of all these kinds of activity, and a plea that we should make better use of them.

An urgent requirement at present is the sketching-in of some *conceptual apparatus* with which the following purposes may be achieved:

(a) to systematise the knowledge we have;
(b) to accumulate further knowledge in significant categories;
(c) to penetrate problems and factors revealed by comparative study;
(d) to rationalise our aims and methods;

(e) to harmonise our purposes, and relate our interests to articulated points of public decision;
(f) to make our recommendations more effective.

Clearly, it will be important to pay close attention to the present complexion, concerns, and possibilities of any comparative study of society as a whole. For the purposes of this book it will be more directly relevant in later chapters to look at what is generally called "comparative education". But at the present stage it may be helpful to look back on the confused tangle of assumptions which we all make when we look at evidence directly before our eyes and attempt to draw generalised deductions or formulae from it. Thus we may help to clear the air, and to rid ourselves of some unacknowledged superstitions. Such superstitions are often wrapped up in scientific language, the rejection of which appears to be one of the most sacrilegious presumptions of our time. Nevertheless, to get at the truth underneath, it may be necessary for us to challenge the ceremonial language, hierarchies, and other impedimenta which prevent us from seeing the plain facts underneath.

Wherever possible, let us use plain language and stop theorising about results. Let us look at simple issues which can be directly observed and tested, without the confusion of dressed-up terminology and ceremonial. Though these methodological axioms are obviously valid procedural rules for any scientific examination, they should be specially insisted on with reference to education. For it is in this realm that almost everyone's perceptions are cluttered up with cant and involved in emotion. All kinds of infantile insecurity hamper any discussion of the need for change. Emotion makes us think that great perennial issues are involved, when a contemporary decision may actually entail nothing more than a change of place or method. Furthermore, so much is involved in our own connection with our past or our children that we tend to think our homes are threatened if the school programme is changed, or an examination altered, though manifestly these are mere matters of expertise which may not in any way affect the principle for which we fear.

Besides, we have all had some experience of education, and most of us have to bring up children; so education often seems to be any man's stamping-ground. So, for that matter, are health, marriage, and earning a living; yet in these concerns we more readily acknowledge the information and advice of specialists who have made a systematic study or important material arrangements which can help us. The inflation of ordinary educational common sense to pseudoscientific nonsense in textbooks and courses understandably makes many lay readers impatient of the "professional" claims advanced in some quarters. That is one reason why it is so important to bring back educational studies into the practical area of scientific and social enquiry outside the "professional" departments, and to use plain language for communicating ideas and information in both directions.

To get rid of some nonsense right away, let us consider the possibility that there may be "laws" of educational development and prediction. Because everyone becomes an educational expert at home, we may begin quite simply with an illustration taken from the family hearth. Any young father who has had experience of putting his children to bed knows perfectly well that a child will resist *his* way of taking the child's clothes off, or the order of procedure he adopts for the bedtime ritual. The child knows the "right" way—mother's way. Custom has all the force of an unchallengeable rule. Most of our etiquette of eating and drinking has acquired a similar force for the same reason. Customs become compulsive. In my own college the members of the senior common room are coerced or chided by such statements as "It is customary to . . ." or "It is not customary to . . .". Examining such a remark, we see that constant repetition (signified also in the phrase "as a rule") acquires coercive if not "moral" overtones. That all happens before there is any question of formulating a "law".

The very word and notion "law" is full of confusion anyway. For all their clear thought, the Greeks used the word *nomos* to indicate "custom", "rule", and "law", although they also had synonyms to give precision to these ideas. Like the Greeks, all of us at some levels of our thought or conversation confuse these ideas, because, though we can define them intellectually, in our looser everyday awareness there is a continuum of emotions and moral sensibilities. The word "law" itself requires very careful examination in our present deliberations, because it has acquired tremendous force during a time of abundant and far-reaching legislation, and has also become associated with scientific "laws". It will help our future reasoning in this book if a few moments can be spent on these and related definitions.[2]

---

[2] For a full but compact analysis of the distinctions to be made when speaking of "laws", see STANLEY I. BENN and R. S. PETERS, *Social Principles and the Democratic State* (London: Allen and Unwin, 1959), Chapters I–III and especially p. 23. It will also obviate excessive regard for "laws" and other supposed forms of direction if we pay careful attention to what is said about "Authority and other forms of social regulation" on pp. 18ff. of the same book.

The classic distinctions of this kind are, of course, to be found in KARL R. POPPER, *The Poverty of Historicism* (London: Routledge and Kegan Paul, 1961) and *The Open Society and Its Enemies* (London: Routledge and Kegan Paul, 1966). Popper makes a basic distinction between the laws of nature (like those of physics), which are unchangeable, and "normative laws" made by man, which can be changed. What he calls "sociological laws" (a term frequently misinterpreted by writers and teachers professing to follow Popper) can be postulated to reveal and *explain* the function of *individual social institutions* which show regularities of behaviour (like the trade cycle), or to reveal and explain *trends* in particular elements of society seen from a single point of view (like population growth). (*Open Society*, I, 67; and *Poverty of Historicism*, p. 118.) But "*trends are not laws*" (*Poverty of Historicism*, p. 115). We can measure and analyse trends in *factors* (but not whole societies or systems) in our attempt to explain them (*ibid.*, p. 126), remembering that such trends depend not on *laws* but on initial conditions (p. 128), or perhaps on the "logic of situations" (p. 149). Any such explanatory statements "always retain the character of tentative hypotheses" which need many severe tests (p. 131). In any case "a statement asserting the existence of a trend at a certain time and place would be a singular historical statement, not a universal law" (p. 115). "The idea that any concrete sequence or succession of events . . . can be described or explained by any one law,

In these secular times we generally recognise that real law is a codified statement of what is required of us, fixing penalties for infraction, and making due arrangements for the punishment of offenders. Such laws are precise, well-defined, *and capable of being changed*. Though we recognise our obligation to obey the law and often feel moral compunction about it too, there is nothing like the feeling of awe or guilt which we experience when we think of our religious obligations. The latter, insofar as we cherish them, are obviously bound up with taboos on a lower-than-religious plane of value; and in the properly religious sphere most of us experience a highly scrupulous regard for the observances of our religion far outside its central commandments. We often feel shock or guilt if we or other people infringe canonical customs enshrined by observance, rather than by laws or formal rules. Nearly all religious people believe in some "absolute" principles which can be more readily discerned and followed by the use of religion than without it. Many non-religious people feel this way too, though they place greater reliance on the use of rational arguments about these principles or their day-to-day implications for human conduct. Nearly all religious believers and rationalists are alike in supposing these "absolutes" and principles to be unchangeable in their essence, and often in their worldly expression too.

Thus they may experience almost the same "moral" shock or sense of betrayal if educational, social, or political proposals are advanced which they feel will ultimately lead back to an attack on the basic religious or rational principles which they

---

or by any one definite set of laws, is simply mistaken. There are neither laws of succession, nor laws of evolution" in the social field (p. 117). Thus, though the "logic of situations" may cause ideas to be acceptable, there is no question of social *determinants* (pp. 114, 139, 143–4, 149, 157, etc.), or of "determining" events in society. Any attempt to distinguish such "determinants" is therefore unscientific and illogical, arising from "misapplied metaphors" (p. 119). (It may be added that Professor Popper fully endorses this summary of his views.)

In any case, I hope to show in this book that there are more helpful ways of construing the development of education, and of studying the factors or considerations which influence *decision*.

cherish, though such proposals may really have nothing to do with them.³ In other words, they hark back to the small child's belief that custom is somehow identified with universal law.

If we look a little more closely at the "laws" of science, we see that these may take several forms and quite different orders of significance. We must, however, be careful to distinguish these varieties of meaning, because so often the significance of one type of law is usurped and applied to other aspects of scientific description or classification, especially in the important matter of prediction. The main outlines can be stated quite simply. Some "laws" relate only to the repetition of phenomena, like the daily rising of the sun, the sequence of the seasons, or the orbits of the heavenly bodies. In other words, the "law" simply states that they have always happened in this particular way.

A second and significantly different stage is reached when a number of associated phenomena are not merely described, but explained on the basis of some hypothesis. This hypothesis is speculation in the first instance; but it can be tested against observation, and sometimes tested by experiment. In other words, this extension of the notion of "law" includes the state-

---

³ For example, the Roman Catholic bishops of Germany meeting at Fulda in September 1960 discussed the Bremen plan for the re-organisation of German schools. They criticised "plans of reform which apparently have as their sole objective the new school organisation", on the ground that if the proposals became law they would have "grave consequences for the world philosophy given by a Christian system of education, and would place in grave danger the very education of the child itself". They pointed out that such a re-organisation of schools, which would keep children together pursuing their different interests in one common establishment and with some elements of a core curriculum shared, would appear to place material or technological interests on the same level with studies more relevant to the "mind". Similarly, Protestant pastors condemned the proposals because "human knowledge no longer is referred back to invariable principles". These references and further details are to be found in M. REGUZZONI, *La Réforme de l'Enseignement* (Paris: Aubier-Montaigne, 1966), p. 80. (Father Reguzzoni is himself a Jesuit priest.) As usually happens in such cases, their Lordships also saw a threat to the freedom of parental choice in the matter of education for their children.

ment of an underlying "force" or at least a tendency which enables an observer to predict certain consequences. Such a "law" manifestly has no logical inevitability (otherwise it would not be necessary to test it and observe it in so many different circumstances); yet a well-attested "law" becomes something on which we can place heavy reliance until new observations or experiments show it to be imperfect in some way.

In the inorganic field (for example, in physics) such general statements of what we can expect become so well proved that they can be almost axiomatic. Nevertheless, the growth of "field theory" shows that even in physics circumstances can alter cases. Furthermore, explanations which seem satisfactory for a very long time may later be shown to be incomplete in their coverage. Thus various phenomena which have been described as waves may later be described as the activities of a particle, or vice versa. Alternatively, a whole new conceptual apparatus (such as the theory of relativity) can account for phenomena on a very large scale, but in a way differing from previously accepted "laws", which are thus reduced to their proper stature as *working hypotheses for further observation*, with tests if possible.

We come to quite a different level of observation and accountability when we enter the field of organic life. Quite apart from the immeasurably increased complexity and multiplicity of material factors involved (such as those in organic chemistry), we usually have to consider the entire physiology of some organism. Perhaps one day this may be more reducible to material explanations than it is at present. At any rate, for the present those explanations do not merit the distinction of being called "laws" with any sense of inevitable sequence, let alone compulsion by force or forces unknown.

Even if we accept the notion of such forces, however, when we deal with living creatures we recognise the extreme multiplicity of interacting "causes" or "forces". These would be astonishingly difficult to disentangle for experimental purposes even in a laboratory. In day-to-day conditions they are further complicated by the life-circumstances of the living creature. This is not merely a matter of the impact of the environment, but also includes the organism's response to the environment—in other words, to the ecological context which is at the very least a two-way relationship. There is constant feed-back. Organisms affect their environment, often permanently. When organisms live together, they collectively establish elaborate patterns of interaction which are themselves the subject of careful academic study on a large and complicated scale, and which in general we call "ecology". One cannot study a plant, let alone an animal, without this intricate kind of dynamic analysis. Thus prediction of what will happen in particular circumstances becomes more intricate.

In the case of the higher animals we are infinitely more involved. Not only do they live in extremely complicated "external" relationships with their environment; they often arrive also at a collective "internal" or "enfolded" adjustment to this environment because of their own gregarious life in communities. Within any community there is a kind of "social" ecology too. Such things as an individual's age, speed, strength, or competence in other ways will help to distinguish what we may call social relationships within such a community. Furthermore, animal communities as a whole perpetuate their success into the future by learning from example and custom. Such methods of communication reach their highest elaboration in the teaching processes which we can observe in our domestic animals as well as in man. It is nowadays recognised that, much further down the animal scale than had previously been thought, all kinds of ceremonial carry weight in this kind of communication. Among animals too, any infraction of ceremonial can produce a feeling of "guilt" or at least of isolation and risk. Such feelings are not to be taken lightly, because they persist at the human level, causing distress whenever alienation or rejection is experienced. They may actually bring about death without any physical cause being added to them. Therefore, it is not surprising that we in our sophisticated society still perpetuate primitive regard for custom, mechanical rules, ceremonial, and the like as well as respect for rational laws or scientifically verifiable hypotheses. We suspect that our *learned* emotions and fears are bound up with inherent "laws", which we go on to communicate to others.

Thus causation and influence are so complex in human affairs that it is quite improper to account for any particular piece of conduct in terms of any precise predetermining "cause". A complex of possible causes may indeed exist, but it would be presumptuous to point to them with any feeling of assurance. As sympathetic parents, as doctors, or as pastors of souls, we may have to make the attempt in an empirical way; but we do not pretend to be scientists when doing so. It is much more a matter of recognising some limits on human responsibility. Moreover, as the phrase "diminished responsibility" reminds us, it is a much safer rule for making verdicts if we resolve to be tolerant of *other* peoples' failings on the grounds of their diminished responsibility than it is to justify our own conduct by the same criterion. Generally speaking, in ourselves we feel that we are fully or mainly responsible for what we do; and the less we feel of "determinism" in our own moral judgement about ourselves, the more likely we are to be satisfactory members of the human community. This consideration has an important bearing on the possibility of direct "cause-and-effect" relationships in human conduct, and above all in the matter of education.

It seems important at this point to stress the immense significance of symbolism in human affairs. As psychologists studying animals have long since taught us, animals tend to perceive their environment in "patterned" ways, and to react to it in behaviour patterns which may be attributed to their heredity or to their upbringing. The determinists would show a direct cause-and-effect relationship here; but the more complex the animal and the environment, the greater the possibility of uncertainty somewhere between "cause" and actual effect; that is, the greater the area of experiment, feed-back, and learning. In human affairs learning is of immeasurable consequence, because experimentation has been done collectively and the results are passed on to us. It is not merely that we have been brought up in certain ways, and habituated to certain customs, rules, laws, and the emotions that go with them; the very ways in which we *perceive* our already highly manipulated environment are patterned in a kind of "language of perception" before we ever begin to think consciously about what is before us.

Whatever there is of instinctive heredity here, there is vastly more of cultural legacy. That is, our upbringing not only has an influence in helping us to absorb certain rules of behaviour or to memorise certain useful items of knowledge; it also has a very considerable influence indeed on the grouping of the objects we observe into some pattern of "significance". For example, we do not merely see plants, or plants to eat (as an herbivorous animal does); we see a garden, or Mr. Smith's garden which we may or may not enter, and we observe that it contains roses in or out of the usual season, and so on and so on. "Patterns of significance" linked with one another, and established in an order of priority, come to us with every waking moment and persist throughout our dreams. We are more "invested" with this language of perception and "understanding" than we are with our mother tongue, which is only one part of the whole order of significance and communication, striking though its influence on our lives undoubtedly is.

So the laws which really do penetrate our human envelope of culture and symbolism (like those governing toothache or hunger) reach out to us not as raw influences but already processed. Their consequences are not quite the same from society to society. In each individual human case they may vary even more than they tend to do from one culture as a whole to another whole culture. Likewise, the more generally predictable patterns of human behaviour, such as the sexual drive or the need for friendship and self-expression, find different forms of expression even generically; and once again in individual cases they may vary even more, because each one of us has his own pattern of symbolism or "ideology" within the general symbolic pattern.

Thus the carefully elaborated patterns which sociologists and other students of human affairs have discerned for us during the past century or so (and which by an extension of terminology can often be described as "laws") tend to be far more relative than universally compulsive. In describing behaviour, such "laws" are usually descriptions of customs or average trends. They deal with *norms* in a purely statistical sense. That is the proper use of the word "norm". Among psychologists it is a joke (though a truism) that not one of us is "normal" in all respects, any more than we are all of average weight, height, colour, or marital preference. At any rate, not all at the same time. Though we may *tend* to follow recognised statistical norms with such sheeplike gregariousness that a norm thus established may become *normative* for us, that is a statement about us rather than about the logic of "cause and effect". The intensity with which we feel obliged to follow the fashion also says something about ourselves individually, and perhaps about our cultural pattern too; but it does not tell us anything about any compulsive "law" in human affairs, as we see by looking at the intense individualism of some countries or families.

The immensely careful studies of society undertaken by demographers, sociometricians, and psychometricians are indispensable to our awareness of what human beings actually do individually or in their community life. The statistical study of human behaviour in its various aspects has become several distinct sciences. At one time each of these tended to follow its individual specialism to the exclusion of what were logically its partners in the study of mankind. But now they are more alerted to their mutual complementariness, and also to social dynamics. Notably, sociology has passed through at least three distinct stages. It once dealt with large single sub-sections of society, such as the Negroes in the United States or the underprivileged people near the starvation line in the United Kingdom; then it proceeded to the micro-sociology of the family, classroom, or workshop; of late is has come to recognise that each one of these tiny elements, painstakingly studied, can only be understood, first, in the immediate context of social relationships around it, and, finally, in the wider social pattern in which it has its being, both laterally and in terms of developmental trends. The whole range of sociological interests is furthermore recognised as being at some points inseparable from psychological, economic, and educational surveys. In other words, we arrive at a situation in which the ecology of any human phenomenon is recognised as extending in a continuum throughout all the constituent and complementary parts of social life—that is, throughout any individual's perception of where he stands, what he is looking at, and what he can do about it all.

Thus a kind of *cultural* dynamic (not necessarily economic or biological), which is hard to measure in plain statistical terms but which is of immense significance, is recognised at last as being a truly scientific concept. The symbolism of which Cassirer so often spoke can no longer be thought to be merely a matter of philosophy or semantics; it is an essential part of scientific appraisal. It is not a coercive law or influence, and in fact precludes the possibility of passive subjection to "sociological laws". The formative influence of this symbolism and our active involvement with it as we build our own lives and perceptions certainly preclude any possibility that the laws of inert physics (relevant to inorganic matter) may be applicable to the study of living things, and above all to the study of such an elaborate and symbolically enmeshed picture as mankind. To some degree all animals are enmeshed in their ecology, which they have helped to create. In the case of man, the situation is infinitely more complex, for man has projected into his environmental relationships and his reconstruction of the world around him not only his physiological and other material needs, but a whole elaborate pattern of symbolism and significance which affects every perception, and which is bequeathed and *taught*.

Some of this complex may be rationally justified, but much of it is pure legacy. That is to say, it may relate to custom, to convenient rules, to sub-rational awareness of various kinds, to codes which once were operable but now are not, or to the systems of material control which man exercises over his environment in the construction of the future. Thus patterns of technological change, and the opportunities which arise from applying technologically produced abundance to social evolution and private energies, all make a vast difference to the applicability of "laws" which we now see to be generalisations from past experience—possibly useful as guide lines for the future but more likely to be of conditional relevance.

Marxists have drawn our attention to these technological influences at work in our society and in personal make-up too; but the symbolism within which we have engaged our lives and personalities, and which is such a profoundly important "language of life" for each one of us, includes very much more than technological processes or compliance with them. Sometimes one symbolism or "culture" retains from the past certain factors or complexes which may have an autonomy of their own (such as schools), and which we hesitate to throw off for the very same reason that we hesitate to throw off our family connections and our ancient taboos. Thus we can no more rely on the single pattern of interpretation derived from Marxism or from statistical "regularities" elsewhere than we can rely on any other single "law" or set of "laws" in attempting to predict the future evolution of human behaviour. Indeed, the Marxists themselves have had to re-think the ancient "laws" of the Marxist prescription, having re-interpreted them according to Leninism and later by the edicts of the Party in whatever country it is operating.

Thus in our study of human awareness we come more fully to recognise the tremendous significance of the overall pattern in which each one of us grows up, and in which each nation or section of a nation has to think out its plans for the future. The "cultural envelope" within which we must try as dispassionately as possible to review our present human condition does not exactly "determine" what we do any more than the basic animal or physical laws determine what we do. Yet if we do not pay attention to it at this stage of our deliberation we are ignoring much of the important evidence before us. A cultural pattern, with all its habits, emotions, priorities, and actual physical apparatus, is an inseparable part of the equipment with which human beings are trying to make their lives. People identify themselves with it. In the matter of education this heritage is more remarkable than in many other areas. All education by its very nature seeks to perpetuate what is supposed to be the best of the past and to provide the growing generation with the best-tried tools for the future. The tools which lie to hand and the preferences shown in the use of them are largely idiomatic.

It did not matter much that the idioms shaping this human equipment varied greatly during the aeons in which human communities were largely separated in mountain valleys or in remote continents. Now, however, the interpenetration of every human life with every other human life, in consequence of the contraction of communications and the immense discoveries of our time, makes it all the more important that we be thoroughly aware of cultural relativity wherever that occurs. Some items may be valid from culture to culture and from time to time. If so, we can find out; and one of the best ways of finding out is to compare assumptions and practices from context to context— that is, from experiment to experiment. In fact, if we arrive at any seemingly workable hypotheses we must constantly re-try it from circumstance to circumstance and from one human case to another.

There are other reasons why this should be our policy. The world is undergoing such rapid change, and labour is so sub-divided (with sub-division of perceptions and senses of significance too), that only *constituent* awareness and constituent competence can communicate relevant suggestions for any study of human affairs. The ancient certainties must be re-construed, and reconstructed in new applications. This is one of the problems of democracy and of democratic education. It is more directly relevant to our present interest if we acknowledge that final answers are hardly likely to be reached for any human problem either individually or within any one culture. The interdependence of mankind and the rapid supersession of many ancient cultures by a "logic" of industrialisation and urbanisation have left mankind very short of signposts, or criteria for that matter. Just as complementary awareness is essential for any enterprise or any community, so, internationally speaking, comparative studies assume unprecedented relevance. Apart from matters of knowledge and awareness, and apart from any consideration of the unprecedented material tools at our disposal, the new roles with which education and government are now invested cannot rely on guidance from any other time, or any other canonical precept from educational textbooks or philosophers. Continuous comparative studies and experiments seem, for the time being at any rate, the most likely way to arrive at workable conclusions.

Why this should be so is fairly obvious. Curiosity about our neighbours is natural, and has been systematically used throughout the history of mankind to gain new information or insights. But comparison is not only for copying, even though it often begins there at the simplest level of enquiry. Observation of our neighbours so as to pick up hints or adopt their devices could be described as one sort of comparison, but that is hardly the sense in which it is systematically undertaken in universities or research departments. The method of comparison used for serious study does, of course, include picking up information, and perhaps hints too; but it is much more a process with the following sequence: skilled acquisition of appropriate items of knowledge; analysis and arrangement of these in meaningful patterns; penetration of the material by comparative analysis; and development of suggestions or hints for policy-making or practice which can be tested domestically and in a variety of comparable external contexts.

For example, all students of language know that words and expressions often change their meaning according to context. As I have said elsewhere, words which seem natural enough (like "mother") change their significance greatly from context to context and from time to time. The same sort of comment applies more obviously still to social institutions, like "marriage", which may at first seem universal. Well-defined terms such as "Christian marriage" vary considerably in social actuality, even though the same church is laying down the rules and conducting the observances, because the faithful in different contexts interpret or ignore the rules so variously. In cases where no universal body of dogma can be called in support, socially contrived ideas like "school" vary conspicuously in scale and significance from context to context, even when we stay within the teacher's frame of reference. When we take account of the extraneous purposes for which schools are used, we notice this truism more markedly still.

In fact, we become aware that words and ideas like "school" or "education" are difficult to confine within a single context at any one time, and therefore their meaning is chimerical. The very fact that they form integral parts of so many social engagements and personal perceptions gives them a great range of interlocking meanings. Each one of these may be analysed in greater depth and with greater clarity if the significance of the idea in various contexts or connections is carefully scrutinised, compared, analysed, and re-tested against observations elsewhere.

This is the kind of knowledge that belongs specially to comparative studies. We acknowledge that a notion like "higher education" or "secondary school expansion" must have several overlapping meanings or embodiments. The structures vary from country to country; and in any one country there may be a particular association with planners' purposes, parental claims, teachers' habits, book supplies, or theories of an educational or political kind. Part of comparative education's stock-in-trade is to know the well-defined types of context internationally, and the common constellations of interest and influence. Moreover, to aid dynamic interpretation of what is observed, great educational issues rise up like waves pushed forward by contributory currents into a great climax—though usually with special characteristics in any one social or cultural situation.

Indeed, the very fact that many forces of an apparently similar kind are sweeping the world to-day (like industrialisation, urbanisation, scepticism, and scientism) makes it all the more important that comparisons be made between one cultural context and another. For example, one cannot study the need for technologists, or the claims of citizens with middle-class standards of expectation, or the needs of the developing countries, without recognising that these are apparently recurring phenomena of a cross-cultural kind. Therefore, we are often tempted to suppose that we observe *the same phenomenon* from context to context, and that the rules of commercial planning, or indeed of physics, may be universally applied here also. To make such a naïve supposition is to ignore the fact that even the uniform articles of commerce—whether they are cows, or cars, or career prospects—are put to quite different social and symbolic uses in different cultural contexts and stages of development. Observing and analysing each one of these complications provides us with one more constituent or complementary part of the necessary information for the study of mankind.

Furthermore, supposing that we think our data firmly established and our perception logical enough, we must nevertheless remember that the other human beings whom we recognise as fellow experimenters in alien contexts are as enmeshed in those contexts as we in our own. They do not start with blank minds any more than we start with unsullied vision. There can be no purely logical transfer of insight or progress. People individually, and peoples seen as cultural complexes, must all make their way towards progress through the institutions and perceptions which they now possess. That is why studies like comparative law, comparative government, and comparative religion exist. The virtue in comparison lies in its recognition that no one system is self-justified, but all are interdependent and perhaps complementary in the insights they give into the *whole* human condition to-day. Though we are eager for more scientific observation and more predictive planning so as to make more productive use of the science and technology at our disposal, we ignore the very essence of any humane or human study if we overlook the inescapable need for continuous cross-cultural and cross-disciplinary observation and analysis.

As was said earlier in this chapter, no area of involvement is more tangled than the field of education. It is still a special area of private emotions, family and social complexes, institutionalised practices and devices, which only recently has become a prime public concern—publicly financed, professionally staffed, and scientifically scrutinised. To try to plan education without reference to the comparative insights referred to in this chapter would be like launching an economic plan with no knowledge of the local intricacies of industry, the corporate organisation of employers and unions, or the internationally available examples from other places. On the basis of comparative education's growing knowledge, already well organised into distinct areas of concern, it is possible to observe and collect data with discernment, to systematise them further, analyse and penetrate them for their hidden significance, and above all to assess them ecologically for their overall "meaning" in cultural context or in time. Nor can we forget the *developmental* aspect of any such study—another matter which abstract theorists often overlook.

This all sounds like a recommendation to let the orchestra play by ear, with only an occasional intervention from an adviser or two in the pit stalls. Far from it. It simply means that to achieve the harmony and still more the symphonic perfection required, a much more complicated competence of interconnected skills is required than would suffice to play an uncomplicated tune on a tin whistle. Nor is it suggested that students of human affairs using a comparative method should lead like a composer or conductor. Scholars in comparative education are themselves players engaged in helping to make a harmony, for which some instrumentation and rules are within their competence. Even this metaphorical statement risks exaggerating their role, for their competence is no more than complementary to that of other students of society. Yet they have their own kind of carefully compiled knowledge, their particularly practised skills, and their special field of sensitivity in an area which they recognise as complementary to that of the other social scientists. There is, however, a transcendent element in their academic make-up: they are not blinkered by the often peculiar circumstances of any country's educational situation at any one time. Unfortunately, most modern planners of education suffer from just that defect, not recognising that educational issues can no more be discussed within the narrow limits of one country's legislative framework than can matters of health or trade. On the other hand, the problems and predictions of education are not amenable to purely speculative "laws" and theories, as though men were molecules or marketable commodities.

Does this mean that comparative studies in education must be a fumbling business at best, or a rule-of-thumb affair? To some degree, yes. All the social sciences are to some extent empirical rather than exact sciences. Greater precision, and a greater chance of reliable prediction or advice, are meticulously sought. This tendency is shown by the growing maturity and academic worthiness of much writing in comparative education. It is further attested in some quarters by reliance on experts in comparative studies who are invited to play a greater personal role in matters of political decision relevant to education. Yet too sanguine an expectation of what can be "scientifically" determined and predicted has made some people overstep the bounds of reliability, especially when they ignore the limitations on objectivity which inevitably hamper any study of human beings working out their aims in complicated cultural contexts. I shall devote the next chapter to the survey of some of these problems.

*two*

# IS OUR STUDY OF EDUCATION OBJECTIVE?

This chapter is a more analytical and penetrating treatment of the reasons why any study of human affairs must rely heavily on a comparative attitude of mind and on comparative techniques. To that extent it is more theoretical. Readers who find it heavy going, or who are already persuaded of the utility of comparative studies, can either dash through it or leave it alone, perhaps returning later. But as a justification for the approach used in this book and as a corrective of some fallacies of theory which can have dangerous consequences when they are applied to practical matters of political or educational decision, the advice given here claims the attention of any student of methodology in the social sciences, and above all of anyone engaged in comparative studies of education. It is not suggested that the ideas presented are new in their essence, though they may be new in their application to comparative education. But even the most seasoned student of methodology in the social sciences generally may do well to consider how tricky the applications of his methods become when the field of research is involved with so many problems of perception, and when the area of decision is so much entangled with the irrational, as the educational arena is to-day.

In all humility let us look simply at some of the words we use. We speak of the "social sciences"—a very fitting description of present studies of society. A moment's reflection teaches us, however, that the word "science" is an extremely imprecise term covering a great variety of activities. There are painstaking observations of carefully isolated data, quantified and analysed in such a way as to facilitate the recognition of general trends within those data, and perhaps of wider patterns. Thus we arrive at hypotheses which can be formulated and tested by further experiment. This is the sort of thing we find in physics and astronomy. There we are dealing with inert matter, as I pointed out when considering "laws" in the first chapter.

Next come the life sciences, as they are now usually called, such as biology and the more elaborate studies of living things. Here observation becomes infinitely more complex by reason of the increasingly complicated nature of the organisms observed. It is far more difficult here to ascribe causation, and as we shall see in this chapter it also becomes infinitely more difficult simply to observe.

Then there are all the "applied sciences" in the field of technology, such as engineering. No competent engineer thinks of himself only as a physical scientist, but insists upon the creativity of his enterprise. In this sense, engineering is not an exact science. This comment is conspicuously more true of applied sciences in the social field, such as medicine. Here we have not only involvement with the biological side of man's activities, but also with all the subtleties of personal relationship between the practitioner and the patient or the public.

As if this ascending order of involvement and questionable objectivity were not enough, we should remind ourselves that our very interpretation of the word "science" almost certainly reflects the confused idiom of our own assumptions. We can see this far more easily when we study words for "science" in other languages. In German, Italian, and Russian, for example, the word for "science" relates not only to the so-called pure and applied sciences of the Anglo-Saxon idiom, but also to all the social studies, academic interests generally, and even the arts. It covers much speculation that cannot be tested. Some might argue that this extension of the term to include hypotheses and theory over a range from philosophy to experimental practicality is justified, though I would not do so. This excursion into semantics is made only to indicate that we must examine the term "science" wherever we use it. It must be analysed before we take our cue from it. To talk of applying the methods of science to the social sciences may indicate no more than the cultural confusion of the speaker.

Yet it might be urged that all the social sciences and all the arts would be better for a more scientific attitude. I fully accept this point of view. The question is what is scientific and what is not. Undoubtedly it is desirable in these days when human roles and perspectives are being transformed by the effects of industrialisation, urbanisation, and other world-wide changes to look for repeatable patterns and for guidance of a statistically verifiable kind. One may also be on the lookout for "laws" or guiding principles for action, if only because any social activity (and especially education) must nowadays be such a carefully planned piece of social engineering. But can all this work be properly described as a science? Can it even be treated as though it were an applied science exactly like gardening or market research? Before we can proceed much further in the discussion of such topics we must look at the whole business of objective perception, and our cultural or emotional involvement in it.

For many of the ideas contained in this chapter I acknowledge my initial indebtedness to A. N. Whitehead's *Adventures of Ideas* (1933). (Several references will be given to this book, quoted from the Pelican edition of 1942.) No one interested in objectivity or in methodology as applied to the social sciences can afford to overlook this extremely penetrating analysis of the way in which our perceptions and ideas are shaped. It is all the more striking to have testimony to our human involvement from a philosopher of such conspicuous intellectual clarity, who was himself a mathematical genius capable of working in fields of the highest abstraction.

Evidence of the highest importance for the purposes of this book is to be found in Whitehead's Chapter XI, which is entitled "Objects and Subjects". Unfortunately some of the language used in that chapter and elsewhere in the book demands such intellectual dexterity on the part of the reader that it seems better here to explain some of the concepts in simpler language, and above all to spell out their implication for our present study. We are shown beyond the slightest doubt that, as he says, "You cannot tear apart minds and bodies"; nor can you dissociate ideas from the institutional context in which they are formulated and brought to fulfilment. Let us look at this now generally accepted contention with the use of some simple diagrams. Though the diagrams are elementary, the concepts which they illustrate are of mounting importance for any would-be objective study of social affairs, and above all for our appreciation of how decisions may be formed.

Subject                          Object

*Figure 1. The supposed relationship of a "detached" observer regarding an object*

Figure 1 diagrammatically shows a person (subject) looking at an object. The person is represented by a black dot, and the object by an X. In casual thought most of us think that this is exactly what happens when we look down the microscope at an object or when we look around at our neighbours. This supposedly neat subject-object relationship is significant enough for casual conversation; but when we look more scientifically at the matter, we see that those simple appearances are deceptive. As Whitehead points out (p. 204), Descartes, Locke, and Hume quite unjustifiably presupposed a complete state of detachment in the observer, and a completely external and inert state in whatever was perceived. Whoever observes or experiences some phenomenon outside himself is both involved in his own background of experience, and, indeed, involved in his relationship to whatever he observes.

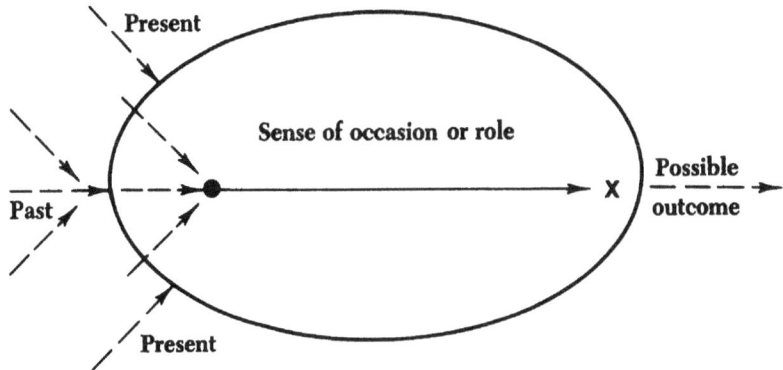

*Figure 2. The relationship between an observer and an object observed on a particular occasion*

Figure 2 helps to make the position a little clearer. It will be seen that the observer (again marked with a dot) is represented as carrying along with him into his perception much past experience and predisposition to see things in a particular way. The dotted arrows also convey the idea that these states of readiness to observe are influenced by the contributions of his upbringing, and encouraged or limited by the opportunities of his environment.

Furthermore, the subject who sees an object is directly or unconsciously aware of himself looking at it. That is to say, a man seeing a fish in a pond looks at it as an angler, as a zoologist, as an aquarist, as an aesthete, or as someone thinking of his supper. In other words, he is conscious of what Whitehead calls "the occasion" of which he himself is a part. That is to say, a great deal more than the transmission of light from the object to the retina goes into anyone's perception of an object. The ellipse shown in the diagram is intended to convey the system or structure of the relationship within which the observer is conscious of observing.

Diagrams are always misleadingly simple; and Figure 2 should be seen to include an element of motion, as suggested by the arrow at the right-hand side of the ellipse. Any real observation, as distinct from a casual glimpse which conveys no meaning, includes some sense of a follow-up in consequence or purpose. This "future" or "potentiality" beyond the object's mere visibility is part of the act of seeing; and Whitehead points out that the observer is often aware of these ulterior possibilities and emotions with much more certainty than he can be said to "know" or recognise objectively the thing he is observing. Thus he says, "The basis of experience is emotional", and goes on to say, "The Quaker word 'concern', divested of any suggestion of knowledge, is more fitted to express this fundamental structure. The occasion as subject has a 'concern' for the object. And the 'concern' at once places the object as a component in the experience of the subject, with an affective tone drawn from this object and directed towards it. With this interpretation the subject-object relation is the fundamental structure of experience" (p. 205).

In much simpler language relevant to the study of society in general, and comparative education in particular, every observation of every kind is highly personalised and also culturally and historically involved. People tend to see things in different ways according to their patterns of culture, to react to them according to the same set of influences and personal preferences, and to make the next move in accordance with a highly idiomatic sense of "what comes next". We all know the feeling "I am looking at this as a researcher—or as a teacher, or as a political animal, or as a protector of my family".

In fact these overlapping senses of relationship involved in anyone's perceptions at any time prepare us to be ready for the next diagram, Figure 3. This should be seen as a kind of

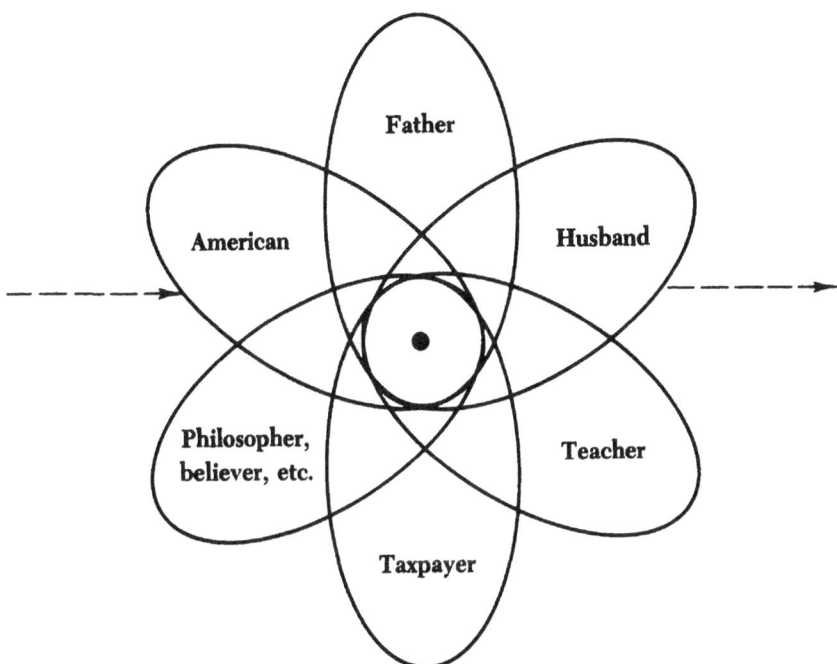

*Figure 3. The part played by roles in influencing personal perception or decision*

extension of Figure 2; but for convenience the object with which we are concerned has been left out of the diagram, although the black dot still continues to indicate the observer or thinker about any problem. The words written in the overlapping ellipses are meant to indicate some of the various roles within which our perceiver sees himself involved. In them he acts out and systematises his personality, making effective and affective contact with the world around him. Through the social or other institutions associated with the various roles, he more effectively pursues his own fulfillment.

Though the diagram is shown as something flat, it could be imagined as a series of structures extending in various directions. These need not always be of one constant size. It is easy to imagine that in family relationships the roles of father, husband, lover, breadwinner, and so on will to some extent coincide; but no one expects a man to behave in exactly the same way towards his wife as he does towards his children. In a harmonious personality the various roles are, of course, complementary and constituent parts of one's life-relationships. In a less well integrated personality, one or more of the ellipses could become disengaged from the others.

Thus the very simple diagram of Figure 2 should really be considered as a part of the far more complicated and interlocking structure shown in Figure 3, equally involved in the perception of any one datum. Any act of supposedly objective observation, therefore, and still more any process of "identifying" supposedly "relevant data", is thus an engagement of a whole personality, with a further complex of social involvement and ideologies. The data's relevance or validity is also largely contingent upon the sense of purpose or scientific discipline associated with the outcome. To pretend otherwise is really unscientific. It does not astonish us therefore to find Whitehead saying "the certainties of science are an illusion" (p. 183).

Perhaps there could have been a closer approximation or homogeneity in what people "saw" at times when cultural patterns remained really standard over a long period and when personalities were made fairly uniform over large sectors of their awareness, as in highly organised religions or in tightly regulated feudal systems. But the more we develop a pluralistic society, and the more completely we become involved in change, the more important it is for us to realise that the various ellipses shown in figure 3 will differ greatly for every individual in each case of observation. At least the size and the outer connections of the loops may be quite different.

Though what is shown here is intended to represent personal observation, the very same diagram with different words (as in Figure 4) could also be used to represent almost any social phenomenon, especially to denote that phenomenon's perception of itself. Let us suppose we are thinking of the notion "school". In this case the dot represents the "personality" of the school, and not the personality of the individual as illustrated in Figure 3. What is represented in Figure 4 is not intended to be appropriate to every single country, of course, for not all schools and teachers are everywhere part of the civil service. Nor are they

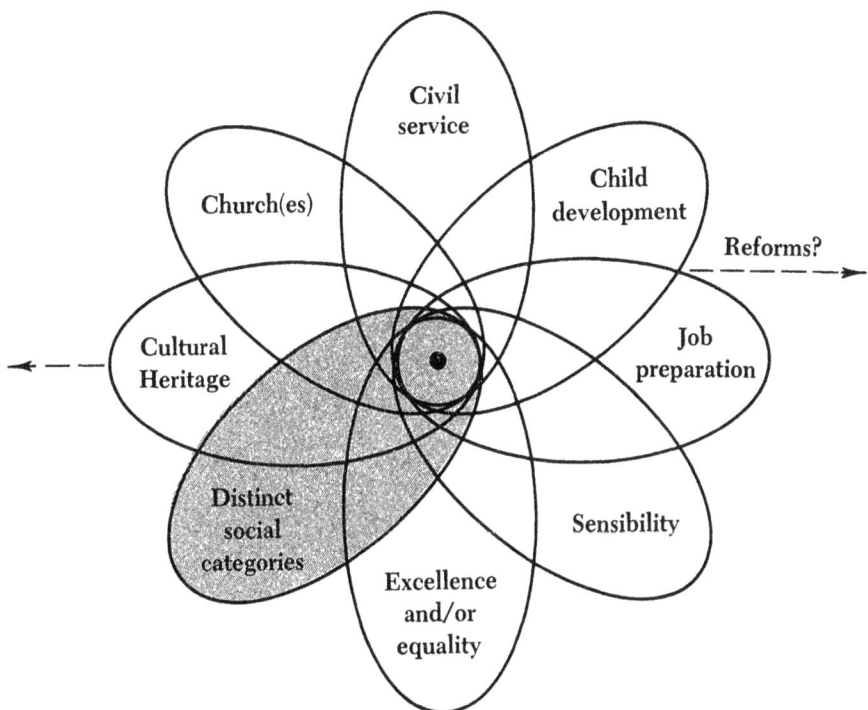

*Figure 4. The "personality" or preoccupations of a school system*

everywhere connected with churches. But we recognise at once that the notion of school in some countries will inevitably produce an awareness of different provision made for distinct social categories. This will doubtless entail a series of differentiated orientations towards examinations or careers and a differentiated supply of teachers. Furthermore, though the school systems of many countries share these attributes generally, the actual features and the meanings of the various distinctions vary considerably from one cultural context to another.

Schools are very much concerned with excellence and the recruitment of talent. Sometimes the main aim is the preservation of cultural heritage. According to each one of these purposes, the notion of school and the emotions it arouses may pull in different directions. There may be a marked tendency towards reform in general, or towards particular reforms. On the other hand, great reverence for the cultural heritage may induce conservatism which regards any change as a menace or as a preoccupation better left outside the schools' purview altogether. The diagram is intended to show only that whatever technical term we use (like "school") has both a personality of its own and also a place in space and time which is not static, but which is inseparable from a developmental dynamic and is often linked with political decisions.

After paying heed to the overall involvement of the notion of school in any one culture, we recognise that despite the contextual involvement of any country's school system there may be some elements which seem to recur from one context to another. The ellipse marked with hatched lines and relating to distinct social categories is one of these. Thus a cross-cultural survey can be made of this particular factor or element, though never in a disengaged way or in any state of objectivity for either the observer or the school system itself—certainly not as far as "laws" and predictions of the type we find in physics are concerned.

Nevertheless, comparisons of a dynamic kind can be made. The name recurs and also the area of concern; but the actual thing we observe and its impact on the surrounding social pattern may be unique. We cannot overlook the dynamics of time and state of development. We shall find, for example, that in some areas distinct social categories are catered for within the one publicly provided school system, whereas in other countries the public system is for paupers and the private system for the elite. The same sort of variation is true for the pursuit of excellence, for relationships with the teachers, or for the involvement of the whole school system in the economy of the country at large. These remarks show that for the proper identification of phenomena related to education, one must always have some model of this sort in mind, not only spatially varied and differentially connected with the context but also differently placed in relation to social movement.

The conceptual models used in this chapter clearly allow for individual variety and for varied kinds of nucleated growth in any one overall cultural context. Therefore they differ greatly from the Marxist interpretation, with its insistence on socio-economic "laws" possessing a kind of infallibility and near-inevitability. The only room for proper variation according to that dispensation is in enterprise shown in adapting one's experiments and personality to the fulfilment or recognition of Marxist "laws". Even that is contained within the envelope of the Party interpretation at a particular time.

The conceptual model used in the present book is far more ecological in its view of human reactions, and far more pragmatic in its view of human involvement with all kinds of instruments and institutions. It is perfectly true that many of these penetrate our lives like the morning ring of the alarm clock or the insistence of a timetable. Punctuality becomes a sort of law for us. To that extent there are transcendent and vitally important cross-cultural influences at work shaping our lives. Some of these, like improved food supplies and medical advance, have world-wide repercussions of a recognisable kind. So do automobiles and the supermarket.

However, the social or personal use of these pieces of apparatus may vary greatly in different parts of the world, for there is always an intervening period of perception during which the new phenomena are interpreted and adapted to suit local conditions or personal policy. Quite rightly we can forecast that the mass-produced foods and clothing now so easily accessible in industrialised countries will very likely lead to a general *embourgeoisement* (or spread of middle-class aspirations and practices) in the population benefitting from them. But there is no inevitability, no uniform response, if only because there is a far greater increase in one's sense of personality in consequence of these aids to self-expression. There is far more variety in clothing nowadays and far richer enterprise in the self-expression of personality than there used to be, despite mass communications and the apparent universality of certain fashions.

On top of all this we should also take account of the fact that social change has turned out in ways that no Marxist canons have been able to predict. The days of property owning among the working class, and the concessions made by employers, not to speak of all kinds of inventions which have raised the expectations of the former proletariat, have all given a twist to the supposedly eternal socio-economic verities at the heart of society. So has the unexpected change in the risks of war. Thus the Marxist gospel has needed constant revision from within the Party itself, to meet changed circumstances both within the fabric of society and in international relationships.

To say the least of it, the whole concept of economic laws pushing the whole conceptual and political apparatus along with a momentum of their own, and with no need for a complement of external criteria, has fallen into disrepute even in the Soviet Union itself. It is not alleged here that the sort of conceptual model sketched in this book would be acceptable to any self-respecting Marxist; but it is noteworthy that since about 1964 at least comparative studies of education and of industrial management in the Soviet Union have acknowledged the idea of complementariness and of "constituent facets of ideology" in a way that would have been unthinkable as recently as ten years ago.

So although each one of the ellipses in the diagrams used in this chapter could be described as "particular ideology" in the sense in which Karl Mannheim uses it in *Ideology and Utopia*,[1]

---

[1] KARL MANNHEIM, *Ideology and Utopia* (London and New York: Routledge and Kegan Paul, Harcourt Brace, 1936), especially Chapters II and III. It will be seen that although Mannheim has much in common with the notions of perception advanced in the present chapter of this book, his use of the concept "determinant" is rather more Marxist and mechanistic than the somewhat biological and experimental emphasis preferred by me. Nevertheless, in the long run, many of Mannheim's conclusions and recommendations reflect a far less mechanistic view than his terminology would indicate. They thus come much closer to my own views than some of Mannheim's phrasing would lead one to expect. One must always bear in mind, too, that Mannheim was more concerned with epistemology and with politics than with the actual apparatus of education, whether institutional or conceptual; therefore, while his observations are always extremely stimulating and have widespread relevance, they frequently need to be re-worked in a closer context of educational discussion proper.

To see how Communist ideology works out in Communist schools, readers may wish to read the chapter on "The Concept of Ideology" in EDMUND J. KING, ed., *Communist Education* (Indianapolis and New York: Bobbs-Merrill; London: Methuen, 1963).

there is not the same sense of inevitability or of a wave sweeping the collective along that one sometimes finds in Mannheim's writing. The conceptual model used here suggests rather that ideas and purposes are invested at any one time in a variously constituted complex of discrete but complementary perceptions. These may occasionally add up to a characteristic profile of "ideology", as we find this in the world outlook of adherents to some of the more authoritatively organised religions. Yet even here we note that the "Catholic outlook", or Buddhism, or Islam may take on highly idiomatic forms of external relationship with the world and with institutions such as schools in the different countries where those apparently monolithic and international ideologies of life are to be found.

It may be noted in passing that the great religions or political ideas of the past have generally confined their major recommendations to a distinct area of human interest, leaving much to the supposedly free area of private choice. Thus religions may have claimed to leave politics, business, and other worldly matters to the individual conscience of the Church member when once he is informed of the great principles and reinforced by the blessings or ceremonials of the Church. Likewise politicians have claimed to keep out of business and science.

More recently, however, material mastery of the universe and the means of production and persuasion too has enabled politicians as well as philosophers to think in more totalitarian terms about the organisation of life and thought. It is important to recognise that attempts will be increasingly made to do so; and it does not greatly matter whether this attempt is made by politicians, businessmen, or other types of planners. Because of the amount of knowledge now available which aids material control, the manipulation of the human beings who now have their lives changed (either haphazard or with some forward-looking perspective) may be to some extent unavoidable.

It therefore becomes infinitely more desirable that all human beings should recognise that no blueprint could possibly exist either in theory or practice which could produce the perfect society or their own particular advantage with anything like the inevitability credited to the laws of physics. It is far more to the point if we let them see that their own perceptions—either through their own "particular ideology", or the ideology of their particular group, or the insights derived from their own particular experiments either in a profession or in the wider aspects of life—are all *active* constituents of understanding. More than that, they are parts of a responsible attitude towards the political process as a whole, being of particular relevance when it comes to decision-making, both in their special circumstances and in relation to long-term decisions for the future.

When planning for schools and other long-term institutions is being considered, inevitably the decisions of to-day may affect whole generations. Thus the importance of pragmatically justified or conceptually valid *contributions to the whole of human perception and understanding* is magnified beyond precedent. The advent of democracy on the heels of industrialisation and mass production, though often thought to be a mass process itself, is more validly envisaged as a kind of apparatus for gathering up into public life and decision discrete but harmonising "ideologies" or emotions—in much the same way as we expect to find them in a well-integrated personality.

Thus we avoid rash dependence upon so-called experts, who are very likely to be experts in one particular field, whereas the enterprise of government to-day should evoke greater participation by the people rather than less. Involvement as conceptualised in diagrams used in this chapter is varied, flexible, and evolutionary. There is no question of subsuming everything into one concentric interpretation such as is advanced in totalitarian states. Neither should there be the kind of obsession with one or more aspects of life which some psychological theorists have manifested, like sex in Freud, or power in Adler; nor should we rely uniquely on one particular set of considerations, a tendency we find in some economists to-day.

We do not need to go far to see that massive ideologies have no room for pervading and persistent influences from other sources than their own pattern of interpretation. They have no place in them for social organisations or sub-groups such as churches or trade unions—or of variously oriented schools, curricula, methods, or even texts. (Even in democratic countries we all know to our cost how these seem to be autonomous and self-justifying, all too often against the trends of the times.) Indeed an all-embracing ideology can see no autonomy anywhere except in "anti-party" form. One of the conceptual problems for a non-Marxist who wants to express our contextual involvement without embracing "total ideology" or "class ideology" is to see how we can formulate our involvement in society in ways which reconcile that commitment with various levels of freedom, and indeed with the opportunity for personal or corporate fulfilment in experimental kinds of self-expression.

A major problem in many latter-day concepts of ideology is that they are so all-pervasive, reflecting their presumption in words like "determined" or "determinants". Their presumption is not only in this quarter, illustrating what Whitehead calls the "Dogmatic Fallacy" of believing that some massive Theory can explain everything definitively; it very often also magnifies Method of a particular kind into a universal panacea. All this reflects the kind of intellectual infantilism which wants to get everything settled and secure—either with no change, or with no loose, inexplicable bits. However, though political decisions and managerial expediency may require clear-cut simplicity of purpose, the truth about the majority of the most important concerns of mankind is to be found in their subtleties and incompleteness. Here we find the growing points of human enterprise, with room for experiment, feed-back, and learning.

At this point we may remind ourselves that all comparative studies, and most researches now intended to make a scientific study of society in any way, are related to the phenomenon of *change*. Prescriptions have seemed perennial in the past. Life patterns have persisted for millennia, particularly for the majority of mankind living on the land or closely associated with it. The Industrial Revolution's implications for our lives, especially when applied in the social field, have changed all that forever,

38   Comparative Studies and Educational Decision

with all the explosive consequences in knowledge and control and communication and expectation.[2]

It would be a pity if human beings, now released from the slavery of agriculture or slavery to machines, were to become the slaves of their own classifications. As we have seen, one may talk about "science" while variously meaning physical sciences, applied sciences, or social sciences, taking up a partisan stand according to the ideology of each and being blinkered to all except its peculiar methods. If we are wise we can use those same distinctive categories to recognise differences of field, of method, and of penetrative powers, without risking divisiveness or making claims to a hierarchical position. We may thus see distinctiveness and yet at the same time interaction. At this point a further diagram may help us to recognise that these three kinds of science may be envisaged as a sort of triangle of interdependent interests and methodologies.

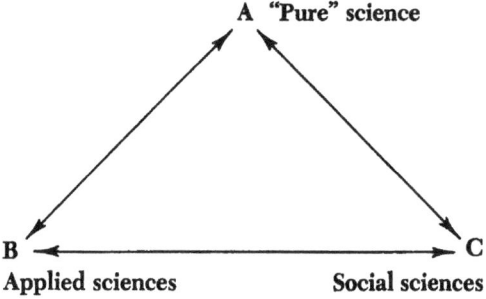

Figure 5.   *The aspects of "science" in relation to social or political decision*

In due course a multilateral or multidimensional model may be thought up; the illustration here is enough for our present purpose. There may be overlapping scientific concerns, and widely appropriate methods; but as a rule it is safer to think of

---

[2] For an up-to-date appraisal of these see EDMUND J. KING, *Education and Social Change* (Oxford: Pergamon Press, 1966), Chapter I.

methods as specific, apart from a few quite simple general principles. It does no harm to characterise much of the present regard for "science" and "method" as to some extent allegorical. That is to say, it is a quasi-mythical representation of something quite simple: that we must be careful in our methods of observation, that we must try to produce verifiable results, and that our endeavours should be productive. Apart from these simple points and others like them, there is no one scientific method.[3] In any case, each of the three aspects of "science" ("pure", applied, and social) introduces new concerns which are tantamount to new problems, as we see on page 46.

It is always more reliable if we seek social truth by implication and approximation as it were, by adding together complementary data or by standing outside ourselves and comparatively surveying other peoples' endeavours. For example, we might note that Soviet attempts at polytechnical and materialistic education have much to be said in their favour when we view them as partial, practical programmes. They are *symbolic* attempts to restore what we know as "learning by doing", or as *l'humanisme du travail,* or as religious regard for the dignity of labour, and they follow the logic of the Industrial Revolution anyway. As a symbolic pattern of presentation to the Soviet people, the polytechnicisation programme in Soviet education is one complementary part of the whole harmony of humanism. No doubt in due course it may be modified, even though to suggest so would seem heretical in some quarters, which we in turn consider to be heretical. That is the whole point about heresies: They run the risk of inflating partial views into universal orthodoxies. Although any human study is bound to be complicated and mobile, the impatient and the insensitive do their utmost to circumscribe us with their specious claims to our compliance with the gadgets of thought or method looking so misleadingly simple before them.

---

[3] J. S. MILL in the nineteenth century imagined there was; but that belief is now rejected by most social scientists and such a scientist-philosopher as Sir Peter Medawar.

Can there be no precision? Can there be no numbers and statistics? Can nothing be quantified and classified? Of course it can. It must be. But it is necessary to note that no one begins collecting evidence at random. There is always an implied hypothesis or pattern. Acquired skills are used to pick up the data, then bundle them together into some classification or *Gestalt*, and later to fit them into some perspective of use. Both the preliminary pattern of perception with which the compilation of data is made, and the methods or processes associated, are all parts of the ellipses in one of the diagrams used here. No godlike Olympian moves metaphysically through an inert world regarding it in some "absolute" fashion *sub specie aeternitatis*. So when we have our demographic details, our computer analysis of trends, or the sort of psychometric and sociometric information provided by the International Evaluation of Educational Attainment, we recognise that we have acquired these data because people had certain prescribed *purposes* in mind, and therefore that the data are "coloured" already. It is precisely at *this* point—not earlier—that comparison begins. It is at this point that the student using comparative method picks up the information he has acquired, acknowledging it to be somehow "impure" and partial. He interprets it by paying attention to the dynamics of conservatism or change which surrounded the gathering of the data, as well as to the dynamics of purpose for which the enquiry was made.

It will be noted that so far we have been talking mainly of academic purposes. Whatever academic conclusions are reached will need to be communicated to nonspecialists or to specialists in other fields. Therefore, in addition to problems of enquiry and of understanding, we confront problems of communication. Our findings are never of unconditional relevance. Our hypothesis of research was coloured; so was our interpretation; so are its implications. They are contingent upon other people's information and professional *decisions.*

It goes without saying that in these days of minute and long-term planning in business, and extremely comprehensive planning by every kind of government (no matter whether it is called capitalist or socialist), our recommendations are not merely communicated to the public at large for prompt and easy decision. They must be to some extent corrected and set in order of priority or perspective by the insights which we theoretical specialists receive from outside. Comparative studies are essential here. In any matter of education we have also to cope with a vast array of indigenous nonspecialists among the parents, and with all the practical problems of dealing with the teachers and administrators. Much depends also on the level of educational enterprise already achieved or required, and the actual possibilities of political and financial decision.

Thus we see that no matter how we oversimplify, or how we magnify our theoretical expertise, we are left in the long run to rely on comparison as a serious academic technique. There are no abstract laws or forces *causing*, or even predicting, events in human affairs. No vision is unsullied, not even of data which we think we objectively observe. Every process of observation has been long rehearsed in accordance with our habits and emotions, not to say the disciplines or techniques which we have relied on. The division of labour which followed the Industrial Revolution and the increasing specialisation which has accompanied the explosion of knowledge make us forget what a tiny facet of the whole our own "clear view" really is. Piecing together understanding cannot be done by vacuum-cleaner techniques or simple accountancy. The process of contributing to understanding must be as humanistic as it is scientific, by recognising the complementariness of all related endeavours. Apparently identical phenomena must be compared before we can be sure of identity, either in facts or in purpose.

The "particular ideology" colouring each facet of perception or "concern" needs to have its significance assessed *in relation to the whole complex* in which it occurs. One particular area or factor (represented by an ellipse in the diagrams) may be cautiously compared with apparently identical influences or factors in another nation's cultural context, as long as we bear in mind the developmental aspect of that whole system, seen in motion and change. Thus if we are talking about the education of girls it is important to know whether we are talking about it in a Muslim country, in Italy, or in the United States; and also to know whether we are talking about 1966, 1936, or 1906. Like good gardeners we recognise the universal importance of certain materials and methods like good seed and good harvesting. At the same time, we recognise that tropical agriculture is not the same as working in a European greenhouse, and that the cultivation of wheat in France is different in many technological and human respects from the same process in the United States. From such homely examples we draw appropriate conclusions for the vastly more complicated field of human relations in education.

It has seemed justifiable to spend all this time on an analysis of why the comparative method is significant for the social sciences, or for any observation to-day, mainly because of the presumptuous short cuts some recommend to us. Clarification is more urgent now because comparative education and other comparative studies can no longer be considered irrelevant academic exercises, but are an inseparable part of to-day's statecraft and political and social decision. In the next chapter we shall look more directly at comparative education itself at its present cross-roads, from which one path may lead to greater social and political significance, while others revert either into the tangle of university scholasticism or to the pettiness of many college curricula.

*three*

# COMPARATIVE EDUCATION: A METHOD OF ANALYSIS AND ENQUIRY

It seems clear from what has already been said that comparative studies are indispensable for any examination of human problems or any evaluation really able to help in making decisions for the future. There are, as we have seen, two main reasons for this: we are by nature incapable of seeing anything with god-like objectivity, but make all our observations through a nexus of social involvement; and, even if we could see some things with detachment, in a world of such rapid and total change there are few signposts from the past. On the other hand, rather than reinforce a point which readers will almost inevitably have accepted before taking up a book with this title and persisting so far with their reading, it may be better at present to consider once again a feature which has been shown to be an integral part of any sustained examination of anything: that such examination includes an element of *purpose* or follow-up implicit in the very question "What is it?" and still more in "What comes next?"

Every child, as part of the most tentative observation, starts to experiment with whatever it observes—touching it, tasting it, and so on. The German expression for "What sort of a ...?" is "Was für ein ...?", implying "What for?" The same sort of manipulative and purposeful questioning persists until we reach the level of the highest academic research. As Sir Karl Popper has shown in his *Logic of Scientific Discovery* and other writings, every scientific observation or discovery is preceded by a hypothesis. This hypothesis is not necessarily formulated; it may be no more than implicit or unspoken. In any case, our sense of individuality or of being external to something that we are examining carries its own suggestion of challenge, to which the observer brings all the armament of habituation or expertise which he possesses. Furthermore, each human being has relative freedom from an obligation to obey his instincts in every detail simply because on the fringe of the instinctual pattern and around the outer edges of our social or personal habituation there are still areas of uncertainty or "growing points". This is the area in which we learn, and sometimes teach. The more we personally learn, and the more mankind collectively learns, the wider the range of possible uncertainties or hypotheses.

To account for any observation, and to "identify" the nature and purpose of a particular object, a multitude of hypotheses may be advanced. The big question is "Which of them makes sense?" More to the point is the question "Which of them makes the most sense?" Largely as a matter of presumption, hypotheses click into place almost automatically as though our brain were a computer previously fed and processed. So it is, in many respects. The more familiar our circumstances and the less changing our environment, the more likely it is that customary patterns of observation and the old rules will seem to give a complete answer for most contingencies. In a deeply rooted rural society, reinforced by religious sanctions and perpetuated in ritual or literature, there may seem to be an answer to everything. Pious Hindus have sometimes told me that in indigenous circumstances in India every occasion of the day throughout the whole of life has a prescription to match. Indeed, there are moments when we all wish this were so. Like the child who knows the way to dress or undress, we all have a tendency to reduce the confusion of life to order and to systematise it. We love to find a rule, a nice undisturbed formula.

Looking back in history or around us now, we can see that primitive peoples imagined they could control or systematise the world by giving everything a *name*. In fact being in possession of someone's name gave a special kind of power over that person. The story of Rumpelstiltskin is a fairy-tale illustration of a supposed "naming power" which every student of comparative religion recognises very well. A rather more sophisticated, but still infantile, temptation is to reduce everything to convenient categories or formulae. We may call them "laws"; but the principle can be the same if we are not careful, or if we feel that the formula has a magic power of also *binding consequences*. The operative formula becomes "deterministic". The history of mythology provides us with plenty of examples. Our human weakness for "binding" formulae is shown in the very word "spell". Enough has been said of these subrational fallacies here. We move now to another aspect.

Having acquired competence and perhaps expertise in one quarter, we are all tempted to believe that this confers omnicompetence. In these days when celebrities shine out repeatedly from every television screen, and when impresarios who have found an "expert" invite him to pronounce on soap or education or morality, it is easy for us to go further astray than ever in the matter of "authority".[1] But no amount of special expertise makes a universal authority. Nor will any single expert method or group of methods serve all purposes. We do not need the diagrams used in the previous chapter to remind us that there is more than one aspect to any discovery or decision. Since

---

[1] Once again the reader is referred to STANLEY I. BENN and R. S. PETERS, *Social Principles and the Democratic State* (London: Allen and Unwin, 1959), pp. 18ff.

we ourselves are so bound up with society, and since there are so many social connections for any decision in this world of expanding contacts, that must inevitably be so. But a further illustration, associated with Figure 5, will help us.

Take the question of the world's food supply, or of birth control, or of atomic energy. In each of these considerations pure science has much to teach us about genetics, or possible insecticides or spermicides, or nuclear physics. Enquiry, therefore, involves at least three facets (information, insight, and decision) in each one of these problems. They are illustrated by the triangular shape of Figure 5. There is the field of pure science and its expertise. There is the field of its application to technology and society. There is also the area of political decision. Between each of these areas of concern there is no direct causative link by which one discovery or event can be said to have sure results in the other. Nor is there a stable hierarchy of importance.

It is extremely important that, while acknowledging the interdependence of these interests and our need for continuing participation by the several experts in concerted discussions which enable the various aspects to be seen in a complementary way, we should be clear about one critical point: there is no certainty of a halo effect of authority or expertise being transferred from one aspect of a problem to another. Neither the expert person nor the expert method can be relied on for omnicompetence. After we have collected and collated all data and advice, the various aspects of the discoverers' and the discoveries' social involvement still require exploratory analysis—and require it afresh as each new problem needs clarification and decision. Quite apart from questions of knowledge or understanding, *decision* depends upon the present context and on the priorities and probabilities to be considered for the future. These all occur in multiple combinations, varying from context to context. That is the whole justification for comparative study—as distinct from the clear-cut decisions for action which may have to be made as a matter of practical politics. And that, as we have seen, is a realm in which we may have little or no expertise.

Even in order to achieve intellectual reliability (as distinct from powers of decision) we obviously need to make use of all the existing resources of the social sciences which penetrate our own field or border on it. After all, they have whole batteries of data which may be relevant to our study—often tested and re-tested by complementary disciplines. They have well-tried empirical methods which have been used for comparative studies of education in only a few instances (for example, at different levels, the empirical work which underlay the Robbins Report on *Higher Education* [1963], and the *International Study of Achievement in Mathematics*, which was published in 1967). Then there are all the methods of "regression analysis", whereby the constituent factors in any problem have been pushed further and further back into the social field where they are isolated temporarily for quantitative measurement. Much of this work has already been done for us, or can now be done better by others. There is no point in keeping our comparative studies at the stage of backyard industry, where we do everything ourselves. The advancing technology or methodology of our comparative interest must increasingly rely on support from the social sciences—from technicians and techniques no less than from top experts and major principles.

What then can comparative studies of education offer in return? There are two advantages which have already been referred to:

(a) a sense of the cultural "wholeness" or "educational idiom" of each area or occasion on which a decision must be taken;
(b) a cross-cultural dimension resulting from the comparison of what seem to be similar factors or problems in a variety of relevant contexts, i.e., in a variety of climaxes.

Thus we arrive at a new two-fold pattern of comparison-for-challenge, in addition to the multiple ellipses and perceptions of Figure 4. I say "challenge" because we are very far indeed from offering certainty. If we were certain, we would not need comparison. What is the point of this challenge? There are several implications. The simplest advantage—but a very important one—is that a series of *hypotheses* can be advanced for further study. For example, the various elements making up a particular problem can be pulled apart and re-assembled somewhat differently, by referring to their different configuration and significance in different contexts.

This theoretical contribution is of such importance in the social sciences nowadays that many serious studies have a "hypothesis committee" (though it may not be called that), whose duty it is to formulate possible assumptions or possible conclusions which are to be tested empirically. Thereupon the "research designers" and the technicians and research assistants can get down to appropriate library work, to empirical enquiries in the field, and to quantitative methods. But concurrently the hypotheses are required to keep the research on the rails—not in terms of techniques or their validation, but in terms of analysis, interpretation, and priority.

Some university or similar research departments have now stopped training their psychological and sociological researchers in all the minutiae of the craft—such as statistical or actuarial dexterity, or skill in preparing data for the computer. Such processes are often better done by assistants; and no harm is done *as long as people keep in touch* and multidimensional awareness is maintained. There is no harm at all in this labour-sharing, any more than there is in having secretaries who do not write well or top mathematicians who are not good at simple sums.

Yet no matter how competently surveys are done, or how well the analyses are done which sustain a piece of advice, no reckoning up of data or considerations compels any particular conclusion. It does not do so even for apparently "detached" theorists; and there is less compulsion still for the person who has to take the practical decision. We all know that there is no inescapable logic about these things; and if there were, human beings are "political animals" and are emotional as well. Besides, in our bookish analyses of contexts which may make us feel we know "the American scene" or some other country's crisis in education, we all too often forget the *developmental scale* along which any social or educational system may be moving. For instance, a country may not have the resources (an obvious point); or it may not have public opinion ready for "the logic" of an appropriate move; or it may still be waiting for the example and experiments of neighbours.

These are all matters in which comparative education can help; but it goes without saying that any findings or recommendations of comparative analysis must be of conditional value. That is, even intellectual evaluation depends upon an ecological alertness to the dynamics of the context. By that I mean the present conjunction of "factors" and the present direction of the local "logic". That is what Popper meant by "the logic of situations". Most influential is *the area for decision*—not necessarily *by* specialists in comparative studies, but I hope with their help. The first help is in clarifying the area of decision.

It is worth pointing out the obvious: the answers given for one purpose now need not necessarily be the same as those given for another purpose or enquiry—not even now. Why then make a naïve attempt to oversimplify things forever by talking about "laws" and predictions? For all the reasons already given, such a proceeding is bound to be of dubious value in practice even if it were admissible in theory.

The reference to Popper (note on page 6) will remind readers how far some writing and theorising in comparative education has wandered from his modern methodology in the social sciences. There is no point in reiterating that for some purposes of social or political calculation one may or must use a dualism distinguishing two kinds of probability—one neat and factual and computable (in single material things), and the other normative and trend-measuring (but in no sense compelling as laws are). After all, this point has been taken—and the point is that it is an argument *against* determinism, not in its favour. For "trends are not laws"; still less are they universal laws. They are only hypotheses which need testing.

By all means we must have hypotheses; but they cannot be formulated in abstraction—only *ad hoc* and in concert with the other social scientists, and in ways which depend on them. Our hypotheses are also subjected to their working-over, even intellectually. After any intellectual conclusion there is always the crux of political and social decision—another thing altogether.

In any case, oversimplified talk about a dual system of "laws" which will be reliable for educational forecasting is to take one of Sir Karl Popper's valuable distinctions out of context. It shows disregard of the symbolic and complicated pattern-making referred to in McDougall's classical descriptions of instinct, which affects our perceptions. It ignores the Gestalt theorists. It pays no heed to what Marx and all the sociologists since his time have indicated to us about the sociology of perception and knowledge. Perhaps we see most clearly what is at stake when we note that this same kind of "law"-seeking methodological dualism is linked with references to "social statics" and social dynamics, in which the safe realm of "social statics" is preferred as a field of research.

Whatever may be possible in other kinds of social study (though I have grave doubts about that possibility), no number of *static* studies of elements of society could really help the work of comparative education. In the first place, nothing is really static in society, and education to-day is one of society's least static elements. Therefore, no quantity of "snapshots" will portray the living whole, with all its "family" significance for its members. Even if we could get a composite moving picture with all the sounds and feelings played into it, it could hardly give us the "inside feeling" of all those areas of decision. Secondly, if such a living picture is to be conveyed, it is probably just as well conveyed by the specialist in comparative education whose field knowledge or on-the-spot experience of a society-in-action can provide hypotheses for others' empirical enquiries of a really dynamic kind, and can help to validate them. This is a scientific relationship that can bear fruit, not an isolated exercise in speculation.

Comparative education is at a crossroads. The big question is whether it is to be an effective and reliably interpretative partner in the social sciences, or whether it is to be reduced to a body of theory (in the narrow sense) which can be *taught as subject-matter* in teachers' colleges—and left there. If comparative education is to be an effective partner in the social sciences, it must go wholly into action with them—offering relevant information, clarifying some issues and suggesting possible causes for events or decisions, suggesting hypotheses or areas for further enquiry, and giving an overall picture of local complexes and transcendent trends. That is the use of comparative education in action. It represents an epistemological attitude widely relevant to our times.

Comparative education has another purpose in *communication*. As no other study can, it informs the general public— and especially teachers—about what education adds up to in a series of relevant experiments elsewhere. Those experiments are relevant because they are other human endeavours to provide likely answers or methods for recurrent problems. Information about all these experiments, reforms, and analyses is sorely needed; and that information is never provided undiscriminatingly as "pure description", but carries some sort of hypothesis or enquiry. It is almost always in some pre-processed or systematised form depending on the degree of competence in the receiver. Its paramount equipment is *comparison:* comparison of contexts in all their significance; comparison of factors, trends, preferences; and *what are thought to be* the outcomes of various decisions in a series of cultural contexts. It deals in approximations and contingencies, not laws.

Of course it is true that certain social data of an apparently objective kind are separately tractable by mathematical means, and capable of being processed by a computer. The kinds of numerical survey already mentioned in the previous chapter are cases in point. But every such analysis or compilation of material, and every act of feeding the data into a computer, necessarily entails some pattern of organisation in the mind of the collector of the data. It presupposes some purpose in the mind of the person arranging the material for the computer.

Quasi-mathematical counting of present facts and the

projection of these into the future inevitably form part of every life and every business, as every act of household budgeting or study of market research shows. We should get nowhere if our food and communications, our supply of books and schools, were not so managed. Likewise, population trends overall lend themselves to mathematical treatment. But when it comes to predicting population trends in a particular country or a particular class there can be no certainty whatsoever. The unexpected is happening all the time. Unexpected factors enter into our wider or long-term calculations. Unforeseen events such as the rise of new nations or war in Viet Nam, and technological factors such as the automobile, atomic energy, and telecommunications, are full of human surprises. Furthermore, if we project the material present into the future on a factual basis, or if mathematical models of future social development are made, our calculations have still to take account of the world workshop of human ingenuity—a labyrinth of possible applications, and a Babel of socially linked "meanings" and pronouncements.

Every newspaper and every television screen nowadays sooner or later shows us a graph of predictions or probabilities in such matters as trade and population. These are essential gadgets of modern thought; but they are only gadgets and illustrative devices. At best they are statements of probability; but more often they are statements of probability *in certain contingencies.* Let one point be clear: they enable us to foresee or predict probabilities; they do not *of themselves* enable us to *control;* and no matter how many reactions we think we can predict, there is *no question of causation.*

It is true that the wide publicity sometimes given to norms or to world events will influence many people in their personal choices if they are keen to follow the fashion; but then it is people who make the movement, and not "causative" events or the statistics set before them. A "sociological law"—if it exists —is a description and not a prescription. It is a hypothesis on present evidence, and no more. The definitions of "law" in Benn and Peters' *Social Principles and the Democratic State* may again be borne in mind here. Furthermore, the complexity of perception, of "meaning", of institutionalised behaviour, and of social or political decision at any given moment, make nonsense of the idea that simple points of decision can be in any sense "determined" in a democratic society, although they may appear to be determined in a state widely using compulsive powers to enforce a political or ideological decision.

This viewpoint appears to be sustained by most modern sociologists as well as by the philosophers quoted; but it is in contradistinction to what Dr. Brian Holmes maintains in *Problems in Education* (p. 53). There he says: "Nevertheless, it shall be repeated, an important assumption of critical dualism is that within any society there are *causal* relationships whose operation can be understood by the establishment of sociological laws. These relationships are functional and constitute a *deterministic element*. It is the study of the relevant sociological laws that constitutes the science of education, or if preferred, the scientific study of education. It is these laws which give predictive power and, *could they be established firmly*, provide the scientific basis of planning". It is true that Dr. Holmes acknowledges that other factors are relevant influences; but his writing shows a marked tendency to talk of so-called sociological laws not only as if they were physical laws, but also as though they carried the compulsive powers of positive law produced by legislation. The following quotation shows what I mean: "A fundamental task of would-be reformers or educational planners is to *establish institutions which will operate according to their sociological laws* in such a way as to achieve stated aims" (p. 79). (The italics in the two quotations above are my own.)

Undoubtedly there are regularities on which we rely to give us our anticipated shape of future trends in single factors or related institutions, especially dealing with material matters. Yet the "laws" referred to by Dr. Holmes and others are no more than descriptions-with-hypotheses. As hypotheses they are shapes *in the observer*, so to speak, rather than shapes in society. They, too, can be changed by human ingenuity, as we see when studying the effects of the Industrial Revolution. Trends do not bear upon human activity directly, but always through the perceptions and institutions with which man has made (so to speak) an "inner ecological envelope" through which he perceives and comes to grips with his environment. Therefore, it is quite inaccurate to pretend that "Such sequences of social events can be stated in sociological laws which bear to man's social environment the same kind of relationship that natural laws bear to his physical environment" (p. 52).

A quotation from Professor H. Stuart Hughes, already referred to in my *Education and Social Change* (1966) puts the objection even more firmly than I. " 'Determination', like 'cause' or 'law', is one of those slippery words that the historian uses only within multiple quotation marks, or in a state of methodological desperation" (in a symposium on "The Great Problems" at Cornell University in April 1965). Reference should also be made to the anti-deterministic views of Sir Karl Popper, quoted on pages 6 and 75, which flatly contradict Dr. Holmes.

We shall do well to remember also what Professor Popper himself has said elsewhere about the process of scientific observation and discovery—that it is always preceded by a hypothesis. That is a statement once again about observers. What we see is what we are ready to see. Furthermore what we observe in human society or in man are largely things of man's making. We hardly ever see them in the raw, if we ever do. We shall be much safer if we regard all alleged laws as hypotheses for a partial survey of some partial aspect of mankind. The great "laws" of the past, as seen in Bentham (that would-be "Newton of the moral sciences"), or Ricardo, Malthus, Darwin, Marx, and all the rest—all these fall back into place as hypotheses.

We are not exactly helped in coming to a precise conclusion about any of these matters because of the confusion in our language at so many points. For example, we often speak of genetic "laws" and a genetic code. Indeed, in a sense we receive at conception some direction or messages that are physical determinants in the literal sense—the so-called "genetic code" which almost automatically processes us over a large part of our being as though we were a punched card in some automatic machine. But this is a *physical* part of us. The only way in which we can talk of a law here is by calling our digestive processes a law or our hormone secretions a law. What we eat and the circumstances and significance of our eating are largely a social matter. Love is inseparable from our hormones; but it is indeed a richly varied harmony manifested in all kinds of social relationships shown in art, music, religion, and philosophy. In any effective sense of the word, love (like language) is learned. Learning can, of course, survive individuals' deaths in institutional form.

Insofar as we talk of a moral code or some other kind of social inheritance, we are speaking of something quite distinct from a genetic code. We are thinking of institutions which have survived, and never died. They retain corporate existence. Individuals contribute to them and receive from them; but the organisation or institution persists. It is a long-lived but acquired habit. If it were not for human imitativeness and wish to conform, the institution would be irrelevant. In time institutions do become irrelevant. They can then be changed or abolished. Statistical norms or the normative examples of a particular time and circumstance also lose their effect, as political development and religious reform show at a multiplicity of points.

Indeed (as many biologists have reminded us) our very personality is largely a store of memories, habituation, half-rehearsed perceptions, and half-conditioned reactions which severally or in groups are brought into play by the social circumstances which evoke them. A man does not always give the same reaction to every woman. Reactions at the dinner table or when dancing are rather different from those in the privacy of the home. All these truisms are of great value for clearing the air when we talk about conditioning and compulsion in human conduct. When we part from what might be said to be biologically or individually conditioned and move into the social field proper, then clearly we must come back to the kind of concept set out in the previous chapter.

Certain methodological consequences follow from this lack of inevitability. When we approach a question on which we intend to do some research or clarification, then we must specify the particular purpose of our interest. We must recognise, too, the associated factors in other interests and disciplines, and the expected future for whatever it is we undertake. There is no one simple method called "problem-solving". It all depends on the kind of problem, the purpose, and the tools at our disposal. Dressing up simple truths in fancy language does not help the matter. Nor, at the other extreme, is it helpful if we too readily "identify" a simple-looking or familiar expression such as "school" or "higher education" in various parts of one country, let alone from one country to another.

It is also important to bear in mind that as researchers we shall not only be examining a problem; we shall be presumably communicating some results. To do proper research we must make it clear at what level we intend to work, and with whom, and with what apparatus. In the matter of communication we should make it clear whether we are talking to other researchers, to university students, to the general public, or to some other group. If we do not do this, we not only hamper our own endeavours but also we run the risk of appearing superficial and unrealistic. In the particular case of comparative education, failure to take into account these important aspects has resulted in some disdain for the subject. At all costs we must avoid "professionalising" or making an orthodoxy of a particular formulation which may, after all, be very ordinary. "Special language" is often one of the sure signs that an institution is on its way to entrenched irrelevance—especially if, as in some educational enterprises, those terms of art and gadgetry turn into subject-matter.

Having tidied up our concepts and terminology, therefore, let us sort out our aims a little more in programme form. Are we looking for facts and relevant data in comparative education? If so, we cannot begin better than with a careful preparation in sociology, including some awareness of the sociology of perception and knowledge. Then we can go on to make careful contextual studies of a richly ecological kind in the field of educational involvement, with reliable perspectives for the future taking account of social and technological change. That is to say, we may do well to know French or American or Soviet education to-day. The whole burden of what has been said so far is that it is nonsense to talk about the first stage of comparative study as being "simply descriptive". The mere act of examination, let alone description, must obviously include a great deal of concept-preparation and also certain working hypotheses. Thus an analytical and evaluative ingredient is inevitably included.

Furthermore, at this stage of enquiry we try generically to categorise cultural patterns as a whole, considering each culture as one idiom within which something is shaped which seems to the inhabitants to be a "world view", or at any rate a sufficient working hypothesis accounting for practically everything that is observed. This is a kind of "inside view" or empathy which I tried to communicate in *Other Schools and Ours*; but that book also traces internationally many implications of technological change and social development for the school systems there described and analysed simultaneously.

Without prejudice to the "personality" and wholeness of that inside view, such a series of case studies inevitably presents some cross-cultural comparisons or contrasts analytically. Among such contrasts are those between centralisation and decentralisation; between intellectualism and pragmatism; between recruiting an elite and socialising the whole population; between advanced and less developed countries. So far from being merely a pleasant excursion, this kind of enquiry and information-gathering through an area study reflects present trends in sociology proper. Sociologists and their academic kinsmen are indeed becoming increasingly self-critical for their "failure" to deal sufficiently with "whole societies".[2] After all, people in any one culture identify themselves individually, and their group or national wholeness collectively, by acknowledging some homogeneity which, despite all their internal diversities, differentiates them from other cultures.

---

[2] EDWARD SHILS, in *Theories of Society*, ed. TALCOTT PARSONS, *et al.* (Glencoe, Ill.: Free Press, 1965), p. 1443.

To make the same point in sociological language we cannot do better than quote Professor Shils once more: "Sociology has not seen with enough clarity that there are properties of societies as a whole that have repercussions on the subsystems. Thus, the subsystems cannot be realistically analysed because their position with respect to the center of society is not taken enough into account".[3] Furthermore, "it is hard for sociologists with their long tradition of studying 'real factors', to appreciate the autonomy of cultural systems and their capacities for autonomous development".[4]

One might go on to say that sociologists so far have tended to take too little heed of the phenomena and significance of *change*, a failing they often share with the demographers, who in any case give us the material rather than the analysis normally required. However, Professor Shils is sensitive to this need and is eager to acknowledge a commitment implicit in sociological studies now, though not always expressed: namely, to recognise the sociologists' involvement. They link the study of culture patterns in any one time and place with the concerns of fellow-citizens who are trying to discern the shape and requirements of the future. Professor Shils's remarkable epilogue on "The Calling of Sociology" in *Theories of Society* is much in sympathy with the recommendations made in the present volume. By the same token, it is a condemnation of the sterile tabulations and "law"-giving still to be found in some writing on comparative education and, indeed, sociology.

Let us further distinguish some of the reasons for a synthetic and comparative interest such as ours. Perhaps our purpose is to see the entire interconnected play of institutions and events making up a cultural system. Or, after acquiring some familiarity with one, we may go on to a comparative research into one particular educational problem. An example might be the comprehensive school in a number of countries, or

---

[3] *Ibid.*, p. 1443.
[4] *Ibid.*, p. 1444.

some aspect of girls' education, or technical education. This is all quite proper to comparative education, and, of course, more specifically pertinent to many present interests than an overall view of what goes on in various countries. But no worthwhile problem-study of a detailed kind can logically come before that overall kind of awareness. Otherwise we mistakenly presume "identification" before we know how what Shils calls the subsystem fits into the social system as a whole. Then we have to consider the time-perspective. Even if our interest were a purely historical and backward-looking one, we could not do justice to our enquiry without the same kind of dynamic analysis of the *evolving* context which, turned to planning, could lead us to study significance for the future.

Indeed, we nowadays readily recognise that whatever we say about any institution (historically considered or otherwise) will inevitably be construed *in the present* and assessed for present relevance by those who read what we write or listen to what we say. Those people also are thinking about the future. We need not be conscience-stricken all the time, yet we do need to be sensitive to our responsibility for social relevance and communication.

In order to clarify to ourselves any issue or problem we have in mind, we should be quite clear that ours is a forward-looking comparative research into a social organism which incorporates both the rational aims and the half-rational involvement of others as well as ourselves. It goes without saying that methods and tools appropriate to this analytical kind of comparative interest are abundantly available, and that they are logically distinct from those of merely learning in general about a whole cultural system. Most of the detailed consideration of comparative education's various stages will be undertaken in Chapter Six; but even at the present stage of preliminary enquiry we do well to acknowledge the many distinct facets of any comparative study.

A frequent reason for enquiry is that someone is following or giving a course in a college as a student or teacher. I have already pointed out elsewhere that this kind of study or teaching is present at various levels, and must inevitably be so. More details will come later; there is no point in labouring the message at this stage. But once again it is clear that the enquirer must spell out what purpose is intended. We can then discover what degree of intensity and what aspect of study will be entailed, with various informative aids of other kinds (such as books, films, or visits); and a suitable order of progression must be envisaged.

There are also other criteria to be considered: whether the comparative study undertaken is to be purely pedagogical or sociological, or whether it is to form part of a literary or an "area study" of the type increasingly found in a number of modern universities. In any such connection more than the usual apparatus of the student of comparative education will be brought into play; for at least a two-way traffic is likely to be established between participants coming from various disciplines. Each one of these considerations will affect our orientation and methods, even if we are solely concerned with comparative education as a method of enquiry. Further criteria are introduced when we go on to consider its use for educational planning and decision.

For there is always the possibility that our enquiry is politically or practically oriented. Now that budgeting for education forms so large a proportion of public spending (which in turn is an increasing part of all national spending), it is important to bear in mind the considerations which politicians or public accountants bring to bear on whatever we say. They are more likely to be concerned with productivity than with cultural values. In a similar way parents and teachers want to know for themselves the brass tacks consequences of whatever new facts or new perspectives we introduce to them.

This aspect of our study is not simply a matter of public relations in the lubricating sense of that phrase. It yearly becomes more necessary for all academic studies to take account of the *public service* aspect of whatever conclusions are reached, even when we are considering only our own methods of enquiry. In any case, teachers, parents, priests, and politicians all want some communication from us. They too are enquirers. We need to use language which will not usurp the role of deciders or persuaders but which will set before others as objectively as possible the materials upon which they can and must make their decision. The recognition that we shall ultimately be held accountable for the production of *relevant* data and *significant* conceptions makes us push back all these considerations to the very moment when we start our comparative enquiry. We must be explicit in our private purpose then, to focus our perceptions. But we recognise simultaneously that we are conducting our enquiries on a public matter of very practical enquiry by others. It is we who miss the point if we ignore our own purposeful context.

A refinement or development of the public service aspect of comparative study (simply for research purposes) is that illustrated by the establishment of a "computable model" to help in forecasting what the expected demand for different kinds of education in the British Isles will be at various stages in the future. A great deal of work of this kind has been done already. More should be done by far. It is not exactly comparative education, but it is the kind of thing without which comparative studies have little meat in them. It is only in very recent years that manpower studies in relation to education, or researches into the costs-and-profitability of education, have been systematically undertaken. Some very promising work is being done in universities and other research departments; notable are those at the University of Chicago, at the London School of Economics, and in the London University Institute of Education.

The volume of work published in these very new areas of academic interest is phenomenal; Dr. Mark Blaug's *Economics of Education: a selected annotated bibliography* (1966) lists 792 titles. The explanatory notes in that book, and published reviews of other books on the economics of education, repeatedly show these facts: that the gathering and sorting of relevant economic and manpower data are still difficult; that the proof of cause-and-effect relationship is in most cases hazardous or nonexistent; that where such a relationship can be presumed it is inseparable in the long run from social and other contextual factors; and that all this sort of thing is constantly in need of evaluation or assistance from researchers or expert commentators in other fields. Among these are colleagues with the insights of comparative education, of sociology, and of industrial development.

All such studies reveal one fact consistently: that you can not leave out the human and the socio-cultural element which so often defies predictability. There is nothing mechanistic about such forecasts. For instance, the excellent work of Professor Claus Moser and his colleagues in the pre-Robbins researches has already been referred to. The researches were a model enterprise in more ways than one, and are continuing in new as well as the old directions. They exemplify meticulous care; but despite the fact that the forecasts were extrapolated from existing trends and based on the resources of existing institutions, the demand for higher education in Britain foreseen and recommended in the Robbins Report (1963) had already been exceeded, year for year, before the time of writing this book (1967), and in the long view the forecast seems likely to fall short of both economic need and social demand.

In fact it is notable that, although the Robbins Report paid much attention to manpower need, its main emphasis was on *social demand*. Surely that must be, in part at least, subject to the vagaries of the surrounding cultural milieu, the intricacies of which have never yet been analysed separately, let alone detailed out for computer treatment. When the whole thing is added up, we realise that the comparative study of education (or educational prediction) is not an exact science at all. At best it relies on the supporting social sciences which are as accurate as they can manage to be—still without giving us mechanically reliable projections or predictions. This they do not presume to do.

Besides, when "predicting" we do not pay enough attention to the known risk of "leap-frogging". This term refers to a frequent phenomenon, most conspicuously found in developing countries which by-pass one or more of the earlier phases of industrial development as experienced by ourselves. For example, they may be shot out of medievalism or worse right into the late twentieth century. In our own midst, too, little account is taken of the "leap-frogging" consequences of automation. By automation I do not mean simply the use of a few computers for electronic mechanisation in a few enterprises, but the widespread use of such servo-mechanisms to control manufacture, distribution, communications, and many of the "service industries" on a nation-wide or international basis. This would (probably will) alter manpower requirements and human relationships profoundly, as the earliest mechanisation did when the Industrial Revolution began. Probably more so.

Therefore, technological change of this order would come immediately into the schools' and universities' area of concern, even in the directly scholastic sphere. In the matter of orientation or of time spent in school and college (or with new devices) the change may be greater still. Obviously, the whole social context of support and expectation would be transformed. Our present proto-automation has shown us that. Sir Leon Bagrit and others have rightly complained about the little thought given to the social and educational meaning of these changes, let alone their consequences.

From all this it follows that predictions in one social or economic sector will help us, but in limited respects. They will not, however, carry the conviction expected from an arithmetical or geometrical exercise. In a complicated system of social or economic interactions, with so many hypotheses to affect calculation, certainty is further away. In any case, school remains a place for human interactions which cannot be automated, even if some supply of information and opportunity can be. Predictions for the wider educational context are vaguer still, and of a more contingent character—never having legislative or statistical certainty or anything like it. In hazarding long-term forecasts we therefore need the concerted and continuous co-operation of colleagues in the several social sciences. They, too, need us continuously. The economist has been trained to think and operate in terms of *quantities,* of investment and jobs and productivity; but the educator retains responsibility for *quality,* and for indicating the likely concomitants of any educational choices.

He knows the way that systems have worked in many contexts.

One postwar consequence of having this mutual need appreciated has been the inclusion in comparative education departments of people with a good sociological or economic background. In a few cases an attempt has been made to establish sociological or research units within such a department; but in many cases co-operation has proved difficult—not always because of unwillingness on the part of the new colleagues, but sometimes because of the inflexibility of specialists in comparative education. Of course, there are notable exceptions. Excellent and profitable co-operation has been maintained in the Comparative Education Center at the University of Chicago, for example. There are others deserving of mention; but to venture on a list would be invidious.

However, if comparative studies of education isolate themselves by becoming too theoretical or too pedagogical, it is understandable that the departments of sociology, economics, and developmental study should build up *within themselves* a "comparative education" interest which owes little or nothing directly to the ostensible specialists in that area. At the time of writing there are two university departments in England which have attracted attention in this way; and there are also particular research surveys (like the International Evaluation of Educational Attainment) which only belatedly or peripherally sought the co-operation of professional specialists in comparative education. Now, however, such specialists (or people with sound comparative insights) are playing a prominent role.

It will be noted that in surveying these later developments we have passed from the realm of purely personal enterprise to corporate endeavour. Team research becomes essential in these days of unmanageably expanding knowledge and unpredictably extending concern. Of course, to some extent knowledge can be "banked" by electronic devices. The same sort of devices can retrieve and disseminate it. The selective retrieval and dissemination of information seem likely to be as important an instrument of public life and scholarship in future as a telephone system is now. Indeed, the two systems may well be linked. But the point that concerns scholarship and its use is surely that this kind of expensive operation demands corporate and *institutionalised* study. Therefore, the way pioneered in intention (though not exactly in scholarship and research) by UNESCO and similar bodies may well give us the shape of academic enquiry and its exploitation for the future.

This kind of thing can already be seen happening in universities. The corporate, continuous co-operation to be found between some African, American, and British universities for the promotion of developmental studies particularly relevant to tropical areas is a case in point. Such joint work, when institutionalised, will doubtless survive its present participants, as it certainly extends their information and "communication value" now. At the University of Sussex there is an important Institute of Development Studies. At Harvard University there is a comparable Center for Studies in Education and Development. At the Institute of Education in the University of London there is a research unit studying educational policy-making; a similar one, with a stronger comparative ingredient, exists at the University of Wisconsin. UNESCO itself has developed a highly important International Institute of Educational Planning in Paris. Doubtless this kind of corporate and institutionalised research with a practical purpose will be of increasing significance for the future shape and message of comparative education. Further attention will be paid to this matter in later chapters, where changes in the nature and commitment of comparative education (in active response to changes in the social and educational perspective as a whole) will be given closer examination.

The effective spreading of concern and participation laterally to "all appropriate others" (as American researchers say) is of the utmost importance for scholarship and social research. Time after time predictions of manpower requirements have severely erred. British postwar forecasts grievously underestimated the scientific and medical manpower needed. Looking back even from this short distance, one can see that the reports erred because they were blinkered by the personal or professional preoccupations of those mainly responsible. More (and more relevant) insights and information were logically called for.

This might have meant a broader committee, which would then perhaps have become unworkable. But just as the commission became a favourite reporting and counselling device from about the 1850's onwards (though it has now unfortunately become a device producing unheeded or outdated reports), so nowadays we need a substitute which will retain similar powers of collecting and analysing and distributing information, but will possess in addition a continuous corporate existence. That need not mean a supercommittee. It could, for example, consist of a computerised and continuous linkage between all research departments and all universities.

After all, whether or not we set up such a pattern of organised collation and comparative analysis, the big businesses of the world and the national or local administrative units are themselves moving noticeably towards it. At a time when "universal" answers or advice are demanded in the field of educational, social, and economic development we cannot escape thinking in such co-ordinated terms. No local idiom or historic device can be very relevant—alone—for internationally useful advice, or even for getting information accurately.

Throughout the world there has been much breaking down of barriers on communication. These opportunities for acquiring and re-construing information do not depend only on new kinds of mechanical communication. They turn on the new realisation that communication across disciplines or between vantage points with different insights depends upon a quite different attitude to enquiry and to teaching responsibilities. This is reflected in new-style universities where old departmental self-sufficiency is called into question or abolished, permitting co-operation within broadly based "schools of studies", and also allowing the provision of "block" or general-interest courses which can be simultaneously followed by students and researchers whose varied personal enquiries or studies surround and contribute to those courses.

Likewise, in several university patterns of reorganisation

the old pyramidal hierarchy under the lifelong direction of one departmental head has been replaced by effective teamwork shared by a number of colleagues whose responsibility for constituent branches of knowledge is both acknowledged and utilised by this means. "Rotating" chairmanships of a department or school are familiar on American campuses, and not unknown now in British universities; but as a rule they are understandably to be found within single departments or "schools". At our present stage of knowledge-building and knowledge-utilisation it is clear that such co-operation may need to be extended far further than is at present envisaged. Cross-cultural and international studies require co-operation of special relevance to the student of comparative education.

When a multifaceted or general-purpose conceptual scheme or "computable model" is being sought for use in a variety of cross-cultural analyses, it becomes more evident than ever that assiduous use should be made of all the information, insights, and resources available to serious scholars of comparative education. They can help not only with hypotheses or evaluation. They are also able to bring missing significance to otherwise dead masses of itemised information, showing likely repercussions in the contemporary systems of education which it is proposed to reform or modify. In any case, unexpected items or facets must generally be added into the reckoning; for school systems have a way of working almost autonomously within a sub-cultural system of their own, which itself interacts through a complicated ecological pattern with the larger educational idiom represented by the national way of life.

The distinctive orientation and methods suitable for an academic enquiry or an overall national appraisal are not quite the same as those adopted to launch a practical *programme*. This is the sort of thing we see in the Nuffield science programmes of the United Kingdom and the corresponding work of the National Science Foundation in the United States. Other excellent examples are to be found in the practice-oriented researches of the Schools Council in the British Isles and in programmes of aid to developing countries. A programme of action is far from being identical with a programme of research, being more closely akin to gardening or the type of social engineering referred to elsewhere. Nevertheless, it is both a proper outcome and a proper beneficiary of comparative study; for like any other innovation, an action programme introduces a new ingredient into an existing ecological pattern or system of social balances. It seems amazing that sociological and economic considerations should be fed into the calculations which surround these development programmes (as they should), while the most obviously comparable considerations (i.e., of education in comparable circumstances) should so often be neglected.

Of course, many such action programmes have a special urgency; and some seem to be of almost entirely domestic concern. But, in any case, it is far better for experimental programmes of this kind to have the benefit of the fullest possible insights. The direction of the programmers is not impaired; nor is there any attempt to usurp the public's right of decision. But what sort of health or agricultural research would be undertaken in national isolation? Comparative education can surely assist and inform decision, though in association with an active programme its methods and communications must clearly be different from those appropriate to the writing of a thesis or to class instruction.

However, international co-operation has necessitated surveys of both practical and academic kinds together. For example, there are such questions as the equivalence of university qualifications in doctors, engineers, or those who wish to leave secondary school to enter a branch of higher education. Then there are questions of content equivalence related to the school curriculum—as distinct from paper qualifications or legal entitlement.

We see this most clearly in the international schools set up to serve the children of those who are international civil servants or employees of major corporations. That was a small beginning; but the growth of the European Economic Community, and the possibility that other countries may wish to join this or similar international associations, at once introduce major and urgent questions of educational decision for which answers may be sought by a comparative survey.

As we progress through these various illustrations of the way in which comparative education and other comparative surveys can be undertaken, we are not claiming that comparative education can make the *decisions* for anyone. It is just that any comparative study must provide relevant data, and communicate relevantly. Unless this last requirement is fulfilled, no one can decide what is feasible; no one can otherwise recognise what is a fallacious or specious argument *ad hoc*, as distinct from a generally valid one, or what order of priorities seem to be desirable. The direction and area of decision belong to the electorate at large or to a Cabinet; but unless the issues and ultimate area of decision are acknowledged, at least in general terms, before ever an enquiry begins, there will be a very great risk that enquiries will be irrelevant by having asked the wrong questions from the start.

In other words, to be scientific in approach, using scientific methods and scientific instruments, we must rid ourselves of the near-theological other-worldliness of medieval schoolmen. We have their counterparts to-day, who deceive themselves with talk about "pure research", "theories", and abstractions generally. All the research into society and perception undertaken for well over a century should leave no doubt that such talk is conceptually unjustifiable and practically abortive. The net result of this latter-day "treason of the clerks" is that the real business of undertaking comparative surveys then passes to other agencies and other kinds of disciplines, without benefit of the painstaking enquiries, knowledge, and expertise so laboriously built up in comparative education.

It is sad to think that this neglect is not caused only by methodological unsatisfactoriness (though that is often serious). Part of the segregation of comparative studies of education from comparative studies of society at large is attributable to excessive reliance on ceremonial or special jargon. Some of us fail to recognise that the concerns of comparative education are also the concerns of other disciplines, which may also have been throwing light on our problems for centuries, if not millennia. Teachers often like to sound magnificent. Their minutiae are made to sound momentous. It is a thousand pities, however, if terminology and methodology become the matter taught or researched into, replacing the actual business and decisions of life. It is these which give rise to the enquiry in the first instance, and will be the ultimate outcome from any satisfactory enquiry.

*four*

# COMMITMENT AND STRATEGY IN COMPARATIVE EDUCATION

In this chapter we move on a stage—from considering comparative studies as a method of enquiry to considering them as a major instrument of public reorientation. That means, of course, directly using an academic study for practical purposes. Thus it may entail taking up the researches and skills of others in a way that directs them to specific purposes of our own devising. Or it may logically demand the inception of new studies acknowledged from the very beginning to have a practical purpose or a probable public outcome. Purists sometimes tell us that research must be free as the air. I suppose some always will be; there is room for poetry in science, and nobody but a Stalin would want to rule it out. But there is also a kind of poetry of conquest—no matter whether the pinnacle to be scaled is Everest or the solution of a desperate human problem. The one concern does not rule out the other, and our problems are urgent. Indeed academic enquiry, like political decision, draws strength from what is "in the air" here and now.

In any case, a book of this kind must take note that, whether we personally want to move from enquiry to the practical use of research findings for public purposes or not, others will. They have done so already, and especially so in the field of comparative education. Our colleagues are concerned not merely with finding things out, but with finding out useful things (as we saw in the latter half of the previous chapter). In comparative education itself the purpose has moved from mainly-enquiry to mainly-reform, or mainly teaching-for-reform, and is specific. What is so very wrong or so very novel about that?

People who are generally contented with their formal educational system, or who experience a vague goodwill towards its evolution, seldom realise how specific schooling has nearly always been. They forget for example, that in the Middle Ages a formal education was nearly always vocational, being directed towards a group of three professions and leaving the others to train and educate their members by apprenticeship or other means. Coming nearer to the present, they may forget the restricted range of social categories for whom formal education was intended—excluding, for example, nearly all girls over a very extensive period, and in many countries to this day restricting the amount of formal education by which girls can benefit. The continuing separation of "secondary" from elementary education in many parts of the world, and the tripartite divisions in secondary education itself, are still familiar to observers in Western Europe. The general conclusion to be drawn here is that formal education as a whole, and the parts of it in particular, were by implication intended for recognisably restricted purposes. Yet the average citizen and the average teacher do not like to have distinctions spelt out in this clear-cut way.

The same kind of specificity is to be noticed in reform movements, or new ingredients in any programme. We notice this in all the remedial introductions into education, particularly in the fields of adult education and vocational education during the nineteenth century. These were often intended to provide a sort of ambulance service, picking up casualties, or else providing correctives to the shortages experienced in the academic diet of the more reputable schools of the time. It serves the general purpose of this chapter to recall that many kinds of institution or programme so introduced experienced a great welling up of vigour and interests as they served topical needs and temper. Then they faded, or else were transformed by adaptation into other enterprises. Thus mechanics' institutes in Scotland and England developed into working men's colleges, while a number of them have finally been transformed into universities.

Linking this information with what was said in previous chapters, we can compare these social innovations in education with the successive flashes of inspiration or the working hypotheses referred to there. Stretching a point, one might talk about topical or social logic for scientific or educational discovery as an evolutionary momentum. That is not altogether a far-fetched comparison, because a remarkable degree of specificity is also found in the evolution of living organisms. Species of fungi attack only particular materials; or they may depend upon extremely precise conditions. Whole ecological communities of varied species which make their lives together respond specifically to changes in the climate or other influences; in turn they actively shape conditions for succeeding alternatives or for a series of dependent organisms. In the *social* life of mankind, however, and still more in our study of the relationship between institutions and practices or theories, we tend to overlook similar ecological contingencies at work. Still more do we ignore the specific nature of social growth and innovation. With the assurance that in recognising these factors we are both humane and scientific, let us go on to see how this kind of specificity can apply to the study of comparative education and of education generally, without loss of regard for such general trends as the development of industrialisation or technological change.

Talk of specific social growth and innovation does not rule out the study of "regularities" in development and experiment. On the contrary, it makes such a study more feasible and logical. More feasible because detailed study of a particular kind of institution in a particular context is very realistic and testable; and even when a transcendent institution (like Max Weber's "Protestant Ethic" or to-day's trend towards comprehensive education) is studied from context to context, both the recurring "regularities" of that particular institution and the challenge of alternative trends or "meanings" in the context can be studied and checked in great detail.

Instead of simply *supposing* that there are regularities—and, still more, regularities operating like mammoth waves—which envelop whole societies with the predictability of laws, we recognise that there may be one or more identifiable and distinct "factors" at work. These may or may not work in harmony, and may or may not have repeatable "meanings" from one context to another. In other words, by being scientific rather than speculative we can observe and analyse educational behaviour and decision by what Popper calls "the method of trial and of *error-elimination*". We can study "the influence of meaning on behaviour" by reviewing the various "arguments" evolved in various institutional contexts. (These are represented by the loops in Figure 4 of Chapter Two; and they correspond to what Popper calls "new organs outside our bodies or persons: 'exosomatically', as biologists call it, or 'extra-personally' ").[1]

Besides, by not taking transcendence or regularities for granted we respect and bring under examination three constituent parts of any comparative study in education: (a) the apparently transcendent organisation, e.g., an evolving type of school; (b) the specific elements or "forces" discernible in the background—industrialisation, urban growth, and "social demand"; and (c) the insights contributed by specialising disciplines—economics, sociology, etc.—to our localised analysis.

---

[1] References here and in the following paragraphs are to KARL POPPER, *Of Clouds and Clocks* (St. Louis: Washington University Press, 1966), pp. 18, 20, 21, 23, 26, and 30.

By paying heed to these varied but complementary parts of any one study, we do not abandon the attempt to understand "regularities" and predictability. In fact, we reinforce such an endeavour by acknowledging that there is more to it than simplistic hypotheses. We share in the vital responsibility for recognising human variety and creativity amidst all the apparent predictability of our behaviour. We discern the multiple "growing points" of experimental *ad hoc* behaviour or hypothesis-making. Popper calls this sort of thing "plastic controls with feed-back", especially when behaviour or ideas have become systematised in institutions.

We recognise, indeed, the overall "consciousness" or meaning to be found in any cultural or educational system; but at the same time we acknowledge the possibility of repeated escape from that overall ideology through the use of new perceptions, new roles, and new criticisms. "Thus we have to be not merely dualists but pluralists" (Popper's reference is to Descartes). That is what "allows us to understand rationally, though far from fully, the emergence of novelty and the growth of human knowledge and human freedom".[2] Our willingness to examine *specific* growth-points and centres of innovation, while heeding the *overall* stock-taking and re-orientation of national or cross-cultural decision, is the very feature that makes us most useful in the decision-making process.

In any case, the majority of people coming to study comparative education, or asking us as persons to help them, do not come with the intention of philosophising about determinism and free will. Nor are they all concerned with the general theory of comparative education. They may have little scholarly interest in world trends in education. They have a specific purpose in mind, as a rule. What is it? Nowadays it is seldom limited to the enjoyment of a kind of academic tourism, at one remove from idle curiosity. It is true that in the past there was a tendency for some educators in well-developed countries to look with

---

[2] *Ibid.*, pp. 26 and 30.

disdain and patronage on the outlandish customs of others. Their reaction may have been one of relief that the observer was perhaps "not as the rest of men". If charity and human sympathy went further than that, the policy was more often to try and convert the unenlightened. In the period since the Second World War we have not altogether escaped from this notion in conducting some programmes overseas; but it is a singularly unproductive enterprise to sell package deals of education.

That kind of condescending interest is not comparative education. Nor is much touristic activity undertaken in its name to-day. It is not strictly a comparative study if we try to find out simply what the Russians are doing in their schools—not strictly, although a comparative ingredient is almost certainly present, to motivate the first mood of enquiry. The kind of uncertainty already referred to in previous chapters must inevitably arise. "How does it all compare with our system?" is an implied misgiving. One might almost certainly presuppose further questions: ". . . and at what points or levels?", and "What can we do about it?"

So even supposedly simple curiosity contains the beginnings of a comparative attitude, especially if it includes any one of the following ingredients: a vague unease which makes one more ready to learn or receive the challenge implied; a wish to know *about* our neighbours rather than simply *what* they do; and most of all, a wish to benefit by the comparison.

In the earliest days of comparative study this kind of benefit was thought to be gained by simple copying or by direct adaptation of a particular institution. Later it was often sought in conclusions from an experiment or experience. The increasing relevance of other people's experience is manifest in a world of change which in some important respects becomes transcendent, as some change clearly does in consequence of industrialisation and urbanisation. We can give examples of changes caused by growing urban or middle-class expectations, and the readiness of young people to stay at school. We can note the eagerness of adults—once "educated"—to alter or evolve their own previous upbringing. All these changes have introduced a note of practicality, and further enhanced the kind of specific or purposeful interest which makes people analyse *problems* comparatively. Such studies are meant to aid decision.

For epistemological reasons and because of recent advances in social psychology we know that this kind of enquiry must always be acknowledged to take place within the ideological framework of our own involvement. Nevertheless, the increasingly purposeful commitment of our study makes us impatient of such intellectual modesty. We want to pass on quickly to special interests which in some ways disturb us. We try to forget the contextual limitations on our work and get down to business. At first sight it seems enough to rely on our researches and the apparatus of our colleagues to supply sharp new insights and instruments of reform; but even if our insights are "right" and our procedures beyond reproach as we penetrate the chosen problem, that is still not enough. We ought also to bear in mind that our enquiry (and still more the implementation of any recommendations we make) depends upon a *climate of readiness* both for the enquiry and for the reform.

This consideration brings us back once again into context. All kinds of elaborate reforms have been proposed only to have their implementation delayed for the passing of two or three generations until the transformation of a country's internal or external scene. Particular instances of this lag in public opinion's readiness to accept the implied logic of educational evolution are to be found in France and England. In 1918 an English part-time day continuation school was provided for in the Fisher Act. After several abortive attempts it finally reached the Statute Book in another form in 1964, as part of an Industrial Training Act. Likewise, the drastic reforms of French education proposed during the period immediately after the First World War had to wait for technological advance to transform much of French society, and for technological need to sharpen political intent. Indeed the Langevin-Wallon reforms aroused bitter controversy as recently as 1946-1947, when they were proposed. It was not until 1959 that they were to a large extent put into legislation, following endemic crises in French politics and education, and under the coercive influence of President de Gaulle. Occasions and topicality can be specific in their influence not only on discovery and decision but on results.

But just as biological species can be grouped into genera, so can social occasions or problems be grouped according to similarity. Without ever losing sight of the inescapable need to refer every decision back to its specific context, one can nevertheless discern some generic tendencies or overall trends. For example, the point has already been made that large-scale alterations of an extremely penetrating nature have overtaken the whole concept and business of education. It is not simply that formal education now has to undertake so many of the responsibilities which were previously dispersed throughout the whole of society or its constituent organisms and skills, though that is true enough. The establishment of formal education as a central apparatus of all of statecraft has already been emphasised. That is the greatest generic change, and many *prima facie* probabilities flow from that.

Publicly streamlined education and world-consciousness, however, do not so much direct the future as make it possible for the members of society to direct their own future. We know so much more nowadays about the nature of man in society. We are more able than before not merely to control the material environment, but to re-organise a society to match our control over physical nature. We also know much more altogether about the nature and workings of education. We have more knowledge about its involvement in society, its efficacy and shortcomings, its formal and informal extension throughout life, both laterally and longitudinally. We are therefore in a much better position to ask *effective* questions and propose possible answers. We are also more able to regulate the fulfilment of our decisions.

The very transformation of the content of knowledge (both material and social) by itself alters the relationship of man to education. It is now a positive, responsible, and lifelong personal-social-vocational involvement not confined to childhood. Education has often been conservative, and been preoccupied with "certainties". Instead of attempting to teach certainties once and for all, we now know that we are involved in a lifelong process of re-learning to cope with uncertainty. Awareness and response both fluctuate. Our stance and our apparatus are unlikely to be fixed (at any rate in material matters). Our concerns are not reducible to any sort of statics whatsoever. This last remark applies to questions of content, method, and value—certainly to questions of commitment and feasibility.

Understandably, therefore, greater reliance than ever is placed on education. Despite the manifest risks of possible unreliability, systematic education is the most humane guide we have. It is the one instrument which we can and must use. At any rate, that is true if education is so systematised and institutionalised as to maintain the best of the past while leaving the future open, not only for matters of educational decision but for political and moral interpretation as well. Thus an "explosion of commitment" with no foreseeable limits in the future extends across the whole panorama of mankind to-day. This global responsibility has altered the entire significance of educational question-and-answer. Let us look at some consequences of this educational transformation. First, the matter of scale.

The familiar expression "explosion of population" originally introduced the question only of numbers of human beings in the world. In schools it introduces supplementary questions about their age range, usually facing us with the pressing preponderance of young people in a poor nation's population. In many countries it has already made the members of the teaching profession the largest single body of employees. When we add into this reckoning the suppliers and overseers of educational apparatus such as books, radio, television, extra-curricular activities, and all the rest of it, the percentage of the population directly engaged in formal education is unprecedented. That is without taking account of the direct participation of people in classes as students or pupils, which is already well over 20 per cent in several countries—even in our proto-technological state of pre-automation. Outside this directly affected population, we must also reckon in the people who feel concerned in it, such as parents and nowadays every elector. In recognition of this change in "concern" we may recall that words like "school" have had rather juvenile or even shabby connotations as recently as the period immediately after the Second World War. At any rate, that was true in Britain and some other Western European countries, though it was hardly the case in the Soviet Union, or the U.S.A., or Japan. The mention of these three countries reminds us that the commitment of education nowadays transcends any national boundaries.

For all these reasons it is obvious that whatever services comparative education could render to the study of education in times before the present must almost inevitably have been on a small scale, or within a restricted purview. The national re-orientation of Japan after 1868 and the purposeful gearing-in of education in the Soviet Union must be excepted from this generalisation. But it is notable that hardly anyone prominent in the field of comparative education had made any extensive survey of Japanese education until relatively recent times; while attention to the Soviet Union has usually been confined to well-marked aspects. It has not strictly been a consideration of its overall lessons for education elsewhere. That appraisal was concentrated on political or ideological discussion, while "education" had only its pedagogical content or its micro-ecology considered.

Nowadays we have learnt that we must reckon not only with pedagogical implications, but with far-reaching repercussions of an extremely important two-way type. Every educational decision at once brings into play a chain reaction of consequences in the social, economic, and, eventually, the political field. We may think we are talking only about comprehensive schools, or some particular structure of university studies; but all our decisions are linked with the present social or job structure of our country, with the nature of economic or intellectual expertise, and with the way in which human beings learn, either individually or in social relationship.

No enquiry can henceforth be made without due calculation of the socio-economic influence of whatever we decide about schools, or without factual awareness and assessment of such influences as the growth of the "service" occupations, and of simply staying on in school. A surprising indication of the change is seen in Britain, where formal education traditionally has been considered largely a voluntary or local enterprise, but where a remarkable transformation has occurred. Indicative of this transformation was the publication in 1965 by the Department of Education and Science of an official report on *Education in the National Plan;* simultaneously massive programmes of research were launched or aided, either through the Schools Council or elsewhere. More recently the Social Science Research Council has fostered fundamental research with a bearing on schools. Voluntary and official programmes of enquiry are carefully coordinated to feed back and measure essential information about trends and influences affecting the whole body politic. Modern research is essentially political in the scale of its significance; but it need no longer be a partisan gathering of bits and pieces. The political significance is too transcendent for that. The outward-rippling repercussions of this new public examination of education can be appraised elsewhere.[3]

The significance of all these considerations for our present purpose is that comparative studies of education necessarily take on a different nature—in scope, in awareness, in fields of interest and methods appropriate to them, and, above all, in their sense of responsibility and strategy.

After this lengthy but necessary preamble, we proceed to see how at different times and in different circumstances studies which were called "Comparative Education" have themselves evolved by notable phases. Hardly any of them have yet taken the measure of responsibilities implicit in any comparative study appropriate to to-day's conditions. There is still far too much contentment with neighbourly curiosity (though that is a useful beginning). There is also too much limitation of interest to the secluded oasis of the classroom and university, and too little

---

[3] For example, Chapters III and IV, "Public Interest—Private Energy" and "Educational Planning and Prediction", in my *Education and Social Change* (Oxford: Pergamon Press, 1966).

attention to educational outcome in the world of activity outside.

Most disturbing by far in my opinion is the limitation of otherwise well-informed writing and public discussion to kinds of enquiry or presentation appropriate simply to teacher-training. That is, of course, an essential and primary responsibility. If teachers are not informed, they may be as much out of date as lamas in Tibet, learned and dedicated in ways which their countrymen or neighbours think irrelevant. It is basic for the progress of education that teachers and administrators in any country see themselves as others see them, if only by implication. Without this kind of awareness there can be no flexibility or possibility of reform. It is one reason why simple curiosity about our neighbours is to be welcomed, though it is to be hoped that it develops as something more systematic. If a climate of some uncertainty can be engendered, that may help educational discernment. But it is not enough. Almost everyone is in favour of reform, in principle. But reform is also a matter of business: it is a matter of decisions, of feasibility, and of effective implementation. That is why comparative education must transcend its hitherto mainly pedagogical character, coming quickly into step with the purposeful but scientific researches undertaken elsewhere—with the sharper perspectives and wider horizons of those other researches.

It will now be profitable for us to look back on the development of comparative education itself. There seems to be little point in trying to give or even summarise the history of comparative education here. That was done particularly well by my predecessor Dr. Nicholas Hans in the first chapter ("Definition and Scope of Comparative Education") of his classic work *Comparative Education*. Some of Dr. Hans's observations have been challenged by the march of events, and by recent developments in sociology and anthropology; but for a historical analysis of the discipline of comparative education his introduction has very much to recommend it. Hans's account had been preceded by Isaac Kandel in *Studies in Comparative Education* (1933), which, though still more out of date in the matter of factual information, nevertheless gives in its introductory part a masterly example of how comparative studies may be systematically and profitably undertaken.

More recently, Professor George Bereday has given a useful historical perspective on the development of comparative studies in the first chapter ("Theory and Method: A General Discussion") of *Comparative Method in Education*. My own interpretation of the present content, scope, and methods of comparative education differs considerably from Professor Bereday's (even in the pedagogical milieu to which he mainly addresses himself). I also feel that his appreciation of the social context and of the methods of enquiry to be used leaves something to be desired; but I gladly accept most of the purport of that first chapter. In particular, I welcome the indications he gives of increasing purposiveness in comparative education and its growing sense of socio-political involvement.

In Professor Bereday's survey we immediately recognise the crescendo of conviction that comparative education must be an instrument of reform. The same evolutionary and reformative interest of comparative education is marked in Mr. Vernon Mallinson's *An Introduction to the Study of Comparative Education* (1957). These writers also stress the increasingly analytical preoccupations of students of comparative education and their general purpose of reform. It is worth recalling that even books which seem to be mainly academic, like Dr. Hans's masterpiece, firmly assume this commitment to practical matters of reform though they do not always spell it out. Underlining this aspect, Mr. Mallinson recalls a crucial quotation from Dr. Hans, declaring that its endeavour is "not only to compare existing systems but to envisage reform best suited to new social and economic conditions. . . . Comparative Education quite resolutely looks into the future with a firm intent of reform. . . . Thus our subject has a dynamic character with a utilitarian purpose".[4]

What Americans call the "immediacy" and involvement

---

[4] Quoted in VERNON MALLINSON, *An Introduction to the Study of Comparative Education* (London: Faber and Faber, 1957), p. 59, from the first volume of the "British Journal of Educational Studies".

of comparative education appears even more strikingly in the pronouncements and writings of such people as Dr. Saul Robinsohn, formerly Director of the UNESCO Institute of Education in Hamburg, and of Mr. Leo Fernig of the UNESCO headquarters in Paris.[5] Looking back, we can see that this reformative purpose and perspective has always been an essential part of comparative study. What has changed is our own awareness: of the world, of education, of the mechanisms through which we contrive the fulfilment of our purpose, and of the repercussions in society or the outside world from whatever we do. Let us then go back and trace the development of comparative education, not merely chronologically but with this evolving dynamism in mind.

One correction which I would suggest to Professor Bereday's historical account may seem to be merely verbal; but it is of great semantic and sociological importance. Professor Bereday says that the first half of the nineteenth century was characterised by the belief that whole "educational systems" could be transposed. Of course Professor Bereday is talking of attempts to transpose *school* systems or parts of them. The only real attempt to transfer or incorporate an entire way of life (that is to say, an educational system in the proper sense of this term) was that of Japan after the Meiji Restoration of 1868. Of course that did not succeed in transplantation, despite the most lavish copying not merely of the apparatus of the West but of many of the concepts and habit-forming systems of the technologically advanced countries.

With this important conceptual correction, it is useful to accept Professor Bereday's general account. The early nineteenth century was a time when many governments became

---

[5] In three addresses given at the University of London Institute of Education in January 1965, Mr. Fernig criticised much work in comparative education as being too static. He earnestly called for more concentration on its developmental aspect, and, above all, for recommendations (like those of UNESCO itself) which can lead to practical programmes—giving them a basis, supporting them, and securing a liaison with empirical research and social evaluation.

aware of foreigners as possible competitors or innovators in the pedagogical field, just as they clearly were in the technological field. Educational innovators or borrowers often thought that they were simply importing a piece of technological apparatus; for the school in those days was very often conceived as a technological adjunct. Professor H. C. Barnard has pointed this out in his *History of English Education,* particularly in describing the monitorial system (p. 54).

It was not surprising that statesmen and leaders of industry and commerce should wish to import apparatus from their neighbours. At the beginning of the nineteenth century Napoleon's success in the military field and his reinforcement of the officer-selection process by his reorganisation of French secondary schools was envied and emulated in Prussia. Various great exhibitions in the nineteenth century also showed prowess which must have depended upon the development of good secondary schools or technologically biased school opportunities. German and French successes in technological and commercial enterprise caused profound disturbance to Britons at the Great Exhibition in the Crystal Palace in London in 1851. Therefore it was not surprising that the profits of that Exhibition were largely devoted to the cultivation of new talents in this applied field on a more systematic basis than previously.

Professor Lawrence Cremin in *The Transformation of the School* (1961) has similarly shown how Russian success in the Philadelphia Centennial Exposition of 1876 caused many Americans to try to inject into their own school systems a better preparation for mechanical and technological expertise. Likewise, at many points of the scholastic horizon one can see a firm determination to observe, study, and, indeed, copy, on the part of men of business as well as of those officially concerned with school processes. Among the latter group Matthew Arnold in England was a conspicuous example, while in the United States Horace Mann and Henry Barnard had been notable. Techniques of teacher training, of using monitorial assistance and all the rest, were freely adopted or adapted.

We sometimes overlook the fact that the importations we

are thinking of were, in the past, between countries with similar backgrounds. Usually there was a nearly homogeneous substratum of culture, institutions, and practices. Notable among these was the influence of various branches of the Christian Church. Organisation along Napoleonic lines seemed reasonable and feasible to regions accustomed to the rule of the Roman Catholic Church and to the example of the Jesuit colleges. A more nucleated and dispersed assumption of responsibility came more easily to those countries with a Protestant inheritance of congregational organisation and concept-formation. Thus the apparently random pattern of picking and choosing (with some discretion even at this early stage) was usually influenced by an underlying state of some readiness.

New problems were occasionally introduced (as in the countries with a large immigrant population, or in missionary countries); but some comparability between the borrowing system and the country copied might often have been presupposed, if only in the minds of the innovators. Moreover, we must remember that in the times of which we are thinking schools were usually credited with only limited-purpose objectives—not global purposes as they are now. We do not now equate education with schools. We recognise that education truly understood means full social and political involvement. We acknowledge that schools are not merely responsive to society, but responsible for much of society's future. In newly evolved countries schools may challenge and entirely transform an ancient way of life.

From there we can go on to accept Professor Bereday's useful statement that such writers on comparative education as Sir Michael Sadler and his successors up to the present time have almost always paid close attention to questions of readiness and compatibility. Metaphorically one might say that they moved on from the inorganic concept of importing pieces of apparatus to the more biological concept of compatibility (as in grafting). Now we have the still more tricky business of considering an entire ecological interaction. By that I mean especially the human levels of social interplay, "symbolic" perception, and value-judgement or emotional decision. This kind of analysis is doubtless what Professor Bereday means when talking of "a speculative treatment of forces responsible for educational practices".

Thus answers might be given to some general questions of administration, school organisation, and so on. Living examples were available elsewhere, which might be in comparable circumstances. Or they might give some indication of why expected results did not follow apparently comparable practices. Thus Dr. Hans devoted scholarly attention to the analysis of background "factors"; and Friedrich Schneider pointed to the "driving forces" (the *Triebkräfte* of the title of his book).

There is always a risk, however, that this notion of "drive" or of "forces" might induce readers and other persons influenced by such writing to think in mechanistic terms. That has certainly happened in some quarters, justifying Professor Bereday's use of the term "prediction" as an ostensible aim of some, though not all, of this earlier comparative work. At a nineteenth-century or early twentieth-century stage of sociological and epistemological readiness, it was not surprising that administrators preoccupied with the developing school systems of their time should have tried to forecast some probable outcomes as though they were planning a kind of factory development, but in purely scholastic terms. (They were then mainly moving on from the mass provision of elementary education to an expanded provision of opportunities in the secondary and technical fields.)

Obviously, we could not now do justice to the development of comparative studies if we confined our attention purely and simply to the school field. The past half century was also a time in which sociological and anthropological studies were developing a wider sense of cultural awareness. Moreover, the rise of new nations after the First World War, often based upon notions of "national character" or cultural unity of some kind (perhaps indicated by a language or some other convenient index of cultural community), made the sophisticated Western world realise that it might also share what Ruth Benedict has called "patterns of culture", more readily recognisable in so-called primitive communities. Much use was made of this concept by Mussolini, Hitler, and the Japanese, and it is now rampant in some newer countries. Nationalism belongs to the political field, of course, though the schools have been brought directly into play.

Then in several countries the churches and other cultural bodies were brought more closely into the arena of educational argument. They no longer confined themselves mainly to the provision of primary education for the masses and selective forms of secondary education for the few. New questions based upon new conceptual ingredients or ideological considerations began to be studied seriously on a large scale, as the churches and others assessed their varied influence upon the developing school systems now being universalised and formalised by official bodies. All this questioning led comparative education on naturally, without a clear break, into what Professor Bereday has called the "period of analysis". Analysis is, however, no longer purely academic. It is more like the dismantling and refurbishing of some old apparatus for vastly more powerful and comprehensive purposes. It is research for reconstruction.

It would not be improper to say that reconstructive analysis is already developing in such a way that we can sort out distinctive purposes and objectives with greater clarity. We are already past the stage at which analysis could be confined to pedagogical or any similarly limited considerations. We have arrived instead at a sense of wide public involvement in any discussion of education today. Clearly those dealing with schools in the limited sense of that concern can derive benefit from the purely pedagogical comparative surveys which some people are still content to do. (I mean, those concerned with school methods, school structure, details of organisation, and the various concerns of the teachers' college.) These do no harm as long as that limitation of purpose does not restrict awareness of genuinely relevant factors, arising from the ecology or environment of the schools. The public involvement already referred to affects every one of the school questions just mentioned, both politically and intellectually.

It is probably for this reason that Professor Bereday has said that some of the most important issues in any educational study whatever must be frankly recognised to be of a political kind. That is certainly true if we consider the word "political" in its wider, Greek sense. The term "political" is useful as a criterion if we think of politics as including surveys of budgeting, of manpower considerations, and of the future structure of society. All these depend to an unparalleled degree upon to-day's schools. Yet that kind of political or business-oriented perspective (practical though it is) does not preclude the use at the same time of sophisticated academic-and-sociological sensitiveness. We began with rather theoretical consideration of our perception-process, of the social organisation of ideas and purposes, and of culture-complexes. Yet the analytical foundation of this book provides a conceptual framework for action—vitally helpful for the future of comparative education. From now on decisions will also need to turn upon more positive and detailed information—some based on new empirical researches, some acquired by co-ordinating and re-appraising existing sources of information.

Just as in sociology it has become extremely important to undertake dynamic studies of *whole* societies (as Professor Shils demanded), so in comparative education it has become increasingly necessary to undertake purposeful studies of whole school systems in action and in process of reform. Hence, there is no question of what Professor Bereday unfortunately calls "descriptive" work. For reasons given in the first two chapters it is doubtful whether such purely "descriptive" work could ever be undertaken. At all events, the new detailed area surveys being published in comparative education are more academically analytical and judgement-demanding than any "descriptive" introduction could be. Several of the UNESCO studies on Africa illustrate what I mean. Studies of Communist education as a whole fall in this category. So does a contemporary series of volumes on *Society, Schools and Progress in* . . . a number of countries. (The present writer is general editor of that series.)

In addition to books written from predominantly educational standpoints, we may list several complementary books with a mainly sociological or economic orientation dealing with whole societies or countries in process of reform or decision; for example, some brought out by the Organisation for Economic Co-operation and Development (O.E.C.D.). Others cover extensive regions either in developing countries or in the more sophisticated world of the Western European Economic Community. On a par with these are studies undertaken by UNESCO or individual countries as a kind of stock-taking or examination of conscience. Several have dealt specifically with particular themes, such as access to higher education, or technological developments in education; attention has also been frequently paid to their social and political significance. Thus many "topic" surveys come within the range of contextual surveys for at least part of their work. Problems of educational decision, political and social questions, and plans for structural reorganisation of school systems are all intertwined with appraisal of the whole collective sense of direction. How then can there be any "pure description" or "pure analysis"? Such language belongs to the nineteenth century or before.

Valuable support for the point of view sustained above (and elsewhere in this book) is to be found in *Essays on Comparative Institutions* by S. N. Eisenstadt (New York: John Wiley, 1965). Dr. Eisenstadt shows that, whereas there had been a tendency for the study of institutions to become separated from the study of attitude-formation or other behavioural processes, the time has come to recognise the interdependence of these two aspects. In his comparative and analytical essays he studies the extent and development of their interrelationships, with particular attention to the *process* of institutionalisation in the modern state, and with reference to the new techniques and information available for such a study. Much attention is paid to movements aimed at changing the social and cultural life of societies, not just formally governmental or scholastic organisations.

There is little new in the interest just noted, taken by itself. It is more significant as indicating where *social and behavioural science* now stands in relation to three distinguishable but inseparable aspects of social development: schools and their organisation or problems; social movements and their influence; political activity and its decisions.

Professor L. A. Cremin in his Horace Mann lecture on *The Genius of American Education* (Pittsburgh: University of Pittsburgh Press, 1965) signalised that "genius" as having gradually perceived the interdependence of society, school, and political purposes in a democratic but intentionally educative society. He established an educational genealogy from Jefferson, through Mann and Dewey, to the educators of the present day. These, he believed, are seeking to make all the great values and perceptions shared in some way by all people in all their variety, while excellence and expertise are pursued by the talented, and while politics or powerfully organised social activity remove the obstacles to a deliberately reconstructive society. Of course, there can be no final prescription—only a more committed attitude to what is involved. But in which way committed? And in which direction?

It is in recognition of the need for more information and insight (into contextual dynamics and interaction as much as anything) that the United States Government is investing so much money in programmes for the study of "international education" or for regional studies of educational development in several parts of the world. This is no idly scholastic survey; it is the proper business of a modern government. The Soviet Union has stopped simply studying "*foreign* systems of education"—a study it has always undertaken; it now recognises that much profit may be derived from more significantly comparative or complementary studies on important topics of common interest. Indeed, co-operation is sought with scholars even in capitalist countries.

The change of attitude in communist countries was clearly shown at a small conference held in Moscow in 1964 to which three English specialists were invited (including myself). The purpose was to review the present status and achievements of comparative education, and to review the possibilities of further development in participant countries as well as internationally. Since then a truly comparative approach has been discernible—one which recognises at least a measure of complementariness in working over problems of universal interest. That change of approach has been shown even in officially approved publications. Notable among these is that of Professor František Singule of Prague—*Educational Trends of the 20th Century in Capitalist Countries (Pedagogické Směry 20. Století v Kapitalistických Zemích*; Prague: Státní Pedagogické Nakladetelství, 1966). This text and the official handout accompanying it frankly make the point that Eastern European countries have much to learn by observing not merely practices but also trends and ideas in the West, while complementary discussions of comparable problems from our side would probably teach us a few lessons.

Considering the once canonical validity for all questions which was once attributed to the Marxist scriptures and to the Party's pronouncements on them, we recognise this as a remarkable move towards a truly comparative attitude. It is not just propaganda talk, either. Eastern European colleagues are more ready to talk, both in personal contact and in learned papers, externally as well as internally where so much re-interpretation is going on. Government by dictation is on its way out, and it has, to all intents and purposes, also disappeared from modern industry in capitalist countries.[6] Executive and administrative decision in business and government alike rests mainly with the collective judgement of technocrats and experts in both situations. Such decision rests more firmly than ever on research and the spread of information—not just information about business or other administration, but on a very wide front of social and international awareness. Educational decision needs this co-operative awareness more than any other field of decision.

Of course, educational co-operation between nations is relatively easy when dealing with some specific programme of studies, or specified technical aid in developing countries, or anything of that nature. An immense amount of this type of work

---

[6] See PROFESSOR JOHN K. GALBRAITH's fifth Reith Lecture, 1966.

is now going on. It is no longer confined to the handing over of money or the loan of experts or institutions, but includes the interchange of views and the difficult business of attempting to formulate policies of a developmental kind. No one likes giving money away without knowing for what it is used. In any case, recent experience of technical development in tropical countries has reduced some long-standing discussions about education and public life to their starkest simplicities. With starvation around the corner and the risk of governmental collapse never far away, problems of priority become more urgent. So do those managerial responsibilities for decision, which, in the development of education, somewhat resemble those of a production engineer in an industrial enterprise. The significance of this type of research into education's involvement has also come home to the more sophisticated countries. Hence the "policy studies" forming an important element of research in several universities, referred to in the previous chapter.

In the previous chapter too it was acknowledged that no false division is now made between theory, research, and practical programmes of either a pedagogical or a developmental kind. Of course the specialised functioning of each type of activity requires its own skills, and sometimes its own personnel. As a matter of practice such activities are often conducted independently. Yet logically all these interests and enterprises are interdependent. Awareness of, and co-operation with, the others is an essential condition of the health of any one of them. In order to do a good job it is necessary for each of the workers in any one of these fields to be honest with himself in specifying which detailed part of the concerted enterprise he is engaged in at any given moment, using materials and methods appropriate to that part. Comparative education's mass of knowledge and equipment of interacting skills may seem a global enterprise when seen generically from outside; but inside it consists of specialising scholars who together maintain a ramification of commitments through co-operation with other academic researches. This complex of interaction distinguishes comparative education to-day from the limited enterprise given the same name in the past. Our overall public commitment is much greater; but individually we specialise more precisely, relying on communication instead of omnicompetence. That communication is not merely with other scholars. It is directly into the field where decisions are to be made.

Looking back, therefore, on our previous preoccupations in this book, we are now in a better position to answer the question asked in the first sentence of the opening chapter: "Why comparative studies?" Three chapters have been devoted to providing a conceptual justification, and to seeing how we find out or re-assemble educational data *in a new significance*. We noted, increasingly, that political considerations also demanded a pragmatic justification. That meant we must go on to consider educational *use*. As we now proceed into the second half of the book, we can discern a working order of *operational* progression. This will continue to take account of what has already been said about comparative education's partnership with many other social studies as an aid to enquiry; but it will re-address itself to those many public practitioners who systematically study education as part of their professional engagement. In Chapter Six we shall pay special and more exclusive attention to teachers and their preparation.

In other words, we now consider not how comparative education has developed historically or can be justified epistemologically, but how it can be programmed as a learning and teaching activity which will eventually feed its students and researchers out into life with the best possible effect. Their preparation will thus be logically phased and productive.

It will help our stock-taking if we again summarise here the main justification for all comparative studies. For in them we can discern the kind of constructive logic which we as teachers try to communicate. The world needs comparative studies and the need will increase for the following reasons:

1. Because every *perception* has subjective "personality" and cultural "socialisation";
2. Because we therefore need to check in various situations and against various criteria of *verification* the perceptions or

"meanings" at which we arrive (which also means working them over empirically in different institutional settings and with different hypotheses);
3. Because the vastly increased amount of knowledge and experience available has introduced *novel insights*, with *new tools of measurement* or observation or experiment;
4. Because increasing sophistication and tolerance have made modern societies more pluralistic, thus accentuating the basic tendency discernible in (2), and extending our concern to include unprecedented *problems of priority* and feasibility, if not value;
5. Because changes in our *sense of control* affect all society, and affect in particular the commitment of education as an *instrument of policy*;
6. Because extension of the Industrial Revolution's logic into the social field has *transformed roles and expectations* for all human beings—both within their national systems and still more in the international field where comparisons are more likely to introduce complementary notions of what is feasible, desirable, or necessary;
7. Because the tendencies noted in (4) and (5) coincide with the need to solve new questions raised by the speed and scope of change, making it impossible to rely on previous criteria or isolated (or "controlled") experiments, and necessitating reliance on widely ranging comparative studies continuously undertaken and *systematically organized*.

Of course, in these circumstances problems of partnership and communication are raised on a scale never before familiar. It becomes more than ever important to avoid omissions or mischances of communication attributable to individual failure. Institutional "bridges" for communication and partnership are clearly necessary, together with all the clearing-house techniques and arrangements for the selective retrieval and dissemination of information which are familiar in modern business. These modern features of educational and social enquiry become more imperative as we move on to consider the collecting of "intelligence" for decision-making, and also the administrative implementation of decisions once taken in principle. These organisational points, however, can be examined more fully in the next chapter, while here we can reflect upon the logic of comparative education's commitment as outlined above.

To advance these reasons for comparative studies is not to claim that only they are worthwhile. Changes in the rationale and method of enquiry imply, however, that previously well-established studies and all kinds of speculation about the condition of man will henceforth be of questionable validity unless they too take account of the kind of logic set out here, to some extent adopting a similar methodology for analysis, and perhaps a similar programme of exposition and decision for teaching and other public purposes, including training for implementation.

This formal exposition of justifying reasons sounds as though comparative studies in general, and comparative education in particular, may be claiming to be all things to all men. In one respect universal usefulness could be claimed—if we limit it to the statement that *comparative attitudes* must inhere in every academic discipline or any human consideration henceforth. That is supported in logic for the reasons already given. But in relation to academic studies and research, the very size and multiplicity of concerns now forming part of comparative education necessitate more than ever the detailed specification of purpose demanded in previous pages. Let us now spell out a few purposes *operationally,* and with reference to teaching rather than to enquiry.

Clearly, new students with little information about the world outside their own country, or about the human ingenuity manifested in manifold ways outside their own profession, can have little awareness of the size and scope of the subject. Therefore they need an elementary introduction, which we obviously call our first stage. Readiness is indicated by the sort of questions constantly asked about the American way of life and its dependence on the schools, or about schools and technological enterprise in the U.S.S.R. In general, it is fair to say that these two countries arouse the most interest throughout the world to-day.

Most of the school systems as we know them now originated on a European basis, largely in Western Europe. Nevertheless, these educational patterns have been elaborated in recent years in both the U.S.A. and the U.S.S.R. in ways which have universally affected school systems and ideas about education—even in conservative countries reluctant to be "Americanised" or influenced by what they regard as undesirable features in the Soviet Union. The interest is undoubtedly there, and it may be cultivated at a fairly simple level of appropriate information.

Other countries too provoke wide concern, especially those usually grouped together as "developing countries". Japan is also included—both for its remoteness, and for its manifest technological brilliance. There is a clear paradox in its unparalleled use of a school system to transform, yet enhance, an ancient and deeply cherished way of life. It is highly important that this kind of simple enquiry should be cultivated. Chapter Six will endeavour to show how this basic curiosity and (so to speak) humanistic approach to comparative education may be made more deeply revealing and stimulate further enquiry. Significantly, books originally intended as comparative texts are now widely on sale as quasi-popular reading, especially in those countries where educational discussion has reached a modest degree of sophistication.

It will be noted that although this first level of "information" is relatively simple, it inevitably includes analytical elements, if only in the guise of hypotheses that are challenged, and often shown to be relative. Besides, all parents and teachers now ask direct questions of a practical kind. Obviously, it is extremely important that teachers should have elementary comparative awareness. They also need, however, some simple comparative equipment for the analysis of their own questions and purposes. For that reason a comparative dimension ought to form part not only of every teacher's initial training, but also of any in-service review of the more specialised problems or techniques on which mature teachers seek advice. Most states of the U.S.A. already require all teachers to undergo in-service training. Likewise, many major corporations in the U.S.A., Sweden, and other advanced countries now require their mature and responsible employees to come back to college for factual up-dating and re-orientation for a rapidly changing world.

At this second and more perspicacious level, information of a descriptive-analytical kind can still be given; but it seems better to raise and *illustrate problems cross-culturally*, or by the varied criteria of different areas of concern (for example, sociology, politics, or business). People charged with school administration (headmasters, headmistresses, and the now massed ranks of educational administrators) also need a constant supply of pertinent information and analysis of relevant questions at this level. Here we have our busy practitioners, technocrats, and executives. But how can we discuss the shape of any country's secondary schools, or higher education, or the problems of linking technical training with professional and humane perspectives unless we do so in a comparative way? Thus we see a well-defined general area of interested activity, which we may designate as a second level for *practical question-raising*. This is especially appropriate to established teachers and to mature professionals who need to be informed, re-informed, or otherwise assisted in their official roles and duties—if not directly in preparation for some decisions.

A third level of comparative education is clearly recognisable as that of positive and purposeful academic enquiry. Such enquiry may be into the domestic concerns of comparative education itself, or into related problems of sociology, economics, psychology, or other social sciences which have a direct bearing on education. This third level is a more systematic world of *research*, in which topics or hypotheses are first envisaged and then limited to one narrow field in which the specialised information or insights of the research worker can secure the maximum penetration. In fact, this is the method most appropriate to the greater part of postgraduate teaching in universities—obviously in the sciences, but more tellingly still in the social sciences. It is in these areas also that the university teacher most notably fulfils his role as a perpetual student. Of course, all research findings are ideally fed back into all teaching or seminars, or filter outwards as advice on practical problems; but there is much frustration of communication here. It is vital for the future that blockages should be removed.

Two points, already touched on, should be repeated in this connection. First, such specialised research has become so refined and so complicated that it is increasingly necessary to rely on the co-operative services of others. These colleagues may be equals working on a related front, or technical supporters and suppliers of information. About four or five of the latter group are usually estimated to be required for each front-line researcher in the sciences. In the social sciences, with their multiplicity of fronts, there is more scope for equivalent and complementary endeavours. The second point is that such team-research seldom takes place nowadays as an isolated nucleus of collective enterprise in a clinical ivory tower. It generally draws upon continuous communication with related corporate enterprises elsewhere. The communications revolution has greatly expanded the notion of "elsewhere". So has the sense of social commitment, which extends to and from industrial or political enquiry into the very heart of any research department. Hence the establishment of national and international clearing-houses and research co-ordinators.

To operate at all at this level presupposes much preparatory information and competence at humbler levels. In our particular field such preparation might be in comparative education proper; but it might equally well be in related social sciences. Moreover, the expertise appropriate to this third plane must for its own verification constantly recall and use the "lower level" information and insight which top researchers are tempted to feel they have left behind. Top-level expertise is logically and practically linked with the daily experimentation and on-the-ground awareness of educational practitioners—even though their theoretical acquaintance with comparative studies is of a relatively simple type. Feed-back has its intellectual value here also. Besides, the political and social implications of any research conclusions in comparative education necessitate this cybernetic kind of communication, if only for reasons of public relations. But it is not simply a matter of publicity, for popular reaction or a contemporary sense of need are important elements to be taken account of in any research study. Thus, the "Olympian" complex is neither practicable nor logical.

Normally, learned research papers and specialised monographs will appear as books or in technical journals. Yet an extremely important informative service of the type mentioned above is performed by popularly intelligible academic journals; for example, *Comparative Education* (published in England), the *Comparative Education Review* (published in New York), and the *International Review of Education* (published in Hamburg). Of course, learned journals in the fields of sociology, psychology, etc., also increasingly concern themselves with comparative studies.

So far I have spoken of three levels of teaching and research enterprise: (1) securing awareness; (2) question-raising; and (3) professional research-with-communication. In what has been said about the third level both here and in the previous chapter, it has become obvious that a continuum of concern exists—particularly between the research aspect and the public service aspect. Later we shall see further generic developments or considerations which need to be reviewed on this plane; but at this point we may give a preliminary examination to a few practical difficulties of a relatively simple kind, caused by the recent expansion of new-style comparative studies which have an advisory or developmental outcome, and necessitate training.

For example, working or advisory conferences cannot be jamborees; otherwise they could never get down to business or would confine themselves to statements of general principles. It may be necessary to limit participation—not for logical reasons but for practical ones. Considerations of organisation and methods are relevant here also. Well-primed and well-trained workers are essential. Likewise, considerations of time and distance become important. Not many people can be given the time or money to travel to India or Africa or some great industrialised city to participate in a "workshop". Still less can they stay in an area as a kind of foreman to guide a programme in action. Yet such on-the-spot follow-up action is just as important as a good beginning—perhaps more so. More permanence and institutional consistency is needed for a fourth level—that of follow-through in development and training.

This fourth level of *developmental* enterprise is growing fast. Without systematic teaching, training, and communication in a well-organised pattern no proper support is available for it. Orientation is therefore needed—both for those undertaking or providing comparative *studies* of development, and also (increasingly) to provide continuous comparative insight or advice to *working* specialists. Among the latter we can number technical advisers, such as agricultural experts or specialists in family welfare, and all those whose responsibilities require them to know how educational patterns of a formal or informal kind fit into their scheme of development for a particular area. In other words, comparative education nowadays needs to canalise some of its enquiries, information, and skill towards support of a directly practical kind. Not to do so is a failure in communication, an abrogation of teaching responsibility.

Writers on comparative education have so far generally failed to take account of this new need in their writing. True, they often help in this kind of work on a personal basis; but most such work is undertaken on an *ad hoc* and hand-to-mouth level, especially when the real specialists in comparative education are compelled by their responsibilities to stay at home and send juniors into the field.

When we consider the extent of developing countries' needs—and indeed the need in developed countries for comparative insights to help the solution of unprecedented problems—it is evidently high time for this newly acknowledged purpose of comparative education to work out its own methods and *institutional* forms—for study and research, for commitment, and for helping decision also. Some of these have been well tried already; but modification and adaptation are called for. Thus, in addition to the three operational levels previously mentioned, we now acknowledge a fourth and most important level: that of public information, with training for development and reform. This commitment is as scrupulous and scholarly as any other learned pursuit. In its own way it is no less dignified and professional than the training of a doctor; likewise, it demands systematic preparation and appropriate institutions. We observe, of course, that the four *operational* stages of teaching and preparation roughly correspond to the four logical stages of enquiry outlined earlier. Further operational discussion of institutions will be given in the next chapter.

In a somewhat random way, but with a continuous thread of interest, this chapter has shown the development of comparative education—historically, logically, and in terms of increasing commitment. The tale is not complete either historically or logically; but it is enough to show that, so far from seeking universal coverage in any book on comparative education or in any definition of the term, we ought to acknowledge that our commitment is now open-ended. No definitive statement of its scope, categories, or methodology is now possible. Any attempt to impose such limitations indicates only the limitations of the speaker.

It is perfectly proper for a specialist to speak with a semblance of authority within the limited range of his own competence or interest. But that authority is provisional, and specialised. In a discipline whose very nature lies in synthesis and complementariness, any tendency to law-giving is reprehensible. It shows unawareness of the present stature of comparative education as a mature but still evolving applied social science especially appropriate to to-day's conditions.

On epistemological grounds comparative studies represent an attitude to enquiry and assessment particularly needed in a time of expanding knowledge and commitment. They are, furthermore, topical in combining scientific logic with humane concern, and in giving a plausible perspective for many related projects for the future. Since education is now inseparably involved in any such project, the comparative study and use of educational activity is constantly necessary—for professional and humanistic reasons. Therefore, any strategy for the future, or any study of the human condition to-day, calls for a new-style comparative study of education which does not diverge from old-style comparative education but is its fulfilment.

*five*

# THE STRUCTURE OF INFORMED DECISION

Ancient patterns of administration were based upon the assumption that a liberally educated gentleman could take thought on everything that mattered and arrive at a universally valid decision. Such preparation as was required could be found in traditional liberal studies, or in the additional use of mathematical concepts and proof, or in a training in logic.

One of the great introductions of the Renaissance was the realisation that experience and experiment also counted. Conclusions henceforth had to be empirically justified and validated by experiment. On the other hand, it took the Industrial Revolution to make it clear that experiences and experiments far beyond the ken of the first decision-makers needed to be reckoned in. That outward-rippling awareness of just how many people's judgement and experiments must be considered has suddenly broken all bounds in our own time. Much talk about democracy, democratic education, and consumer consultation is an acknowledgement of that realisation.

Yet in one important respect the conclusions we draw from our present state of awareness tend to be archaically "liberal". That is to say, we often imagine that once communication in some conversational or journalistic way is assured between the rulers and the ruled, all will be well. That is tantamount to supposing that, given this latter-day type of revelation, the well-poised deciders of our future will once more come to the right conclusions and ensure their fulfilment. However, all around us we hear comments which make us suspect a catch somewhere. Non-economists complain that economists behave as though they were "touched by the Holy Ghost". The other social scientists insist that there is more to planning than one-way revelation; and even economists on the west coast of the United States have been heard to complain that they cannot understand the language and concepts of their colleagues on the Atlantic coast. So once again we are brought back to the matter of discussion and complementariness.

The communication of ideas does not simply happen. One of Karl Mannheim's most important contributions to sociological thought was his insistence that ideas take shape and are fostered only in appropriate *institutions*.[1] Indeed, Mannheim, who was a Jew, attributed the immense success of Christianity to its achievement in incorporating many of its ideas and teachings in fostering institutions. Mannheim was not, of course, the only thinker to develop this point; but in our own time he became the most conspicuous person linking this notion of "institutional thought" with plans for the development of education through involvement with the structure of society.

In all this Mannheim was the inheritor of Robert Owen, who early in the nineteenth century realised that no profound educational or social change could be achieved without the

---

[1] See particularly KARL MANNHEIM, *Freedom, Power and Democratic Planning, passim.*

corresponding re-organisation of the structure of society to match and foster new ideas. More recently the Owenite hypothesis had been taken a stage further in the United States, notably by such people as Jane Addams and William Wirt. Jane Addams did not merely say, "Unless all men and all classes contribute to a good, we cannot even be sure that it is worth having". She also sought to revitalise social creativity with appropriate institutions, mainly educational settlements. Such champions of reconstructionism brought a needed note of practicality to the more vaguely progressive enthusiasms of directly pedagogical innovators such as John Dewey.[2] Thus Dewey's vaguer insistence that a democratic society must be "intentionally educative" was already linked with reconstructionist notions of a more overtly political or socio-economic type.

On the English scene, the same awareness of a need for institutional change to back up and foster educational and civic growth was to be found in the writings (and still more the addresses) of Sir Fred Clarke, a close friend of Mannheim. The deaths of these two men unfortunately halted the discussion of institutions as matrices for ideas, at least with reference to education. Certainly there is plenty of room for discussing institutional reorganisation and reconstruction, not only as Professor Theodore Brameld does in the United States, but with special reference to their epistemological and decision-guiding role.

I mean by this that information processes need to be meticulously studied and empirically organised in institutional form. There is no time for understanding to form like a cloud of gossip in the market place. Information cannot quietly flow along the lines of commerce. It is too complicated to be identified with personal and social intercourse. Nowadays knowledge is made. It is manufactured, distributed, stored, and selectively retrieved by mechanical methods which almost rival the marvels

---

[2] Further reference to these influences on the development of American education can be found in my *Society, Schools and Progress in the U.S.A.*, (Oxford: Pergamon Press, 1965), pp. 114 and 195ff.

of the human brain, and work much faster. Certainly, the collective mass of information available far exceeds the capacity of the most Baconian polymath.

One consequence of all this change is that there can be no true-false decisions. In future our way of life requires real "multiple choices" of an extremely multiple kind. Yet we remain unaware of the data, the significance, the likely consequences, the instrumentation, and all the necessary factors for our judgement unless we have been fed with these requirements systematically through an institutional pattern of communication. Otherwise we are out of touch with the intelligence necessary for our "strategy of decision".

So much must be evident for epistemological reasons alone. But by daily observation we recognise that hardly any public decisions concerning national policies for education really take place as though a long-term strategy were involved. At best we see local tactics, not strategy. Yet many such decisions involve legal, financial, and institutional re-organisation which may condition (if not determine) a school pattern for generations. That is, such decisions immediately take institutional shape; but the institutions derived from such decision may be ill-conceived and work against the logic of our times or our international realities. This consideration alone makes it clear that we cannot take once-for-all decisions in an airy nineteenth-century fashion. All decisions affect structures, and they are in turn affected by structures. It is urgently necessary for systematic studies to be made of the structure of informed decision in the literal and metaphorical senses of those words.

It seems doubly important to emphasise this point here, for since the Second World War the ancient arrogance of "liberal" thinking about how decisions are arrived at has been matched by a kind of "empirical" arrogance which matches it. Obviously we need information, and the more that information is testable and quantifiable, the more reliable it sometimes is, and the more easily it is packaged and stored. No one would believe more readily than I that more information of a reliable kind is required. But there is a tendency to believe that only quantifiable and empirically achieved information is worth while. This extreme is no more acceptable than a purely "liberal" extreme. As we have seen, all empirical and other enquiries are preceded by a hypothesis; and it is possible for that hypothesis to be seriously misconceived, or *socially* inapplicable. One example will suffice. The elaboration of intelligence tests led to some remarkable doctrines about the intelligence quotient (IQ). Educational thought was trapped by these hypotheses and techniques. For quite some time in English educational circles the nimble handlers of statistics and the manipulators of tests in vogue were the only "respectable" authorities on education, and quickly possessed themselves of leading professorial chairs.

Unfortunately for them and for the future development of English education as a whole, educational studies and curricula and university departments of education in Britain became organised in such a way that it became almost impossible to pay effective heed to alternative studies of education or indeed admit their relevance. Sociological influences on "intelligence" were ignored. Though sociological studies are now highly respectable, comparative studies are still considered to be mainly of a peripheral relevance. Any sociological studies are of the micro-sociological kind, which may serve the local tactics of special decision, without greatly assisting the more important strategy of major educational, social, and economic decision. This is the type of failing which Professor Shils and others have sought to correct in the books already referred to.

In any case, what about all the other questions and all the other factors which ought to be considered? Mr. H. L. Elvin, Director of the London University Institute of Education, has several times drawn attention to important omissions. In particular the following quotation will help: "But is the only admissible evidence what some research workers choose to call 'facts'? And are we to call research only what has been experimentally conducted? (In English the word 'research' has strong overtones from the physical sciences and the use of it in complex human situations, like those of education, can have a distorting effect unless the research worker is highly sensitive and, even more important, practical minded rather than doctrinaire)".[3]

Besides, what is in question here is not only information or the findings of research; it is the process of discussion and decision. Much information is available but unincorporated either intellectually or institutionally. Even if it were so incorporated, the nature of present-day changes is such that arrangements need to be provided for *continuous discussion and continuous review*. Indeed, it is clear that major decisions to-day must represent a kind of "continuous creation", no matter what may have happened in the past. The decision-making process itself must frequently be firm enough when major questions of legislation, finance, and manpower planning are involved. Nevertheless, situations change so fast that a continuous review seems necessary. There is nothing surprising about this notion when we see that in urban architecture, in commercial organisation, and sometimes in school building, the possibility of continuous re-adaptation is built in.

The acknowledgement of built-in obsolescence and institutionalised provision for reform is not novel; but it is largely unheeded. Yet we do well to remember and profit from the example of some university or research degrees in other countries. For example, the qualification awarded by the Atomic Research Training Centre at Saclay in France becomes obsolete after five years. Surprising though this news is at first, it may well be a prototype for recognised obsolescence during decades to come, not merely of degrees but of organisations. The example may be

---

[3] *Paedagogica Europaea*, (Amsterdam and London: Agon Elsevier, W. R. Chambers, 1966), p. 237. This article is valuable in pointing to false hypotheses raised by economists and others, and to the misleading nature of concentration on what is readily quantifiable, especially where questions of quality or special circumstances are involved. Such corroboration of the point of view sustained in the present volume is all the more valuable for coming from a leader of the enquiries into higher education which resulted in the Robbins Report of 1963, and the director of a centre for so much empirical enquiry.

carried beyond the field of theoretical qualifications and practical research into the institutional field where educative significance has been taken for granted or ignored. In other words, it may well be that within the foreseeable future formal provision may be made—may have to be made—for continuous review and continuous re-organisation of public decision, executive follow-up, and institutional implementation in order to meet the exigencies of a world changing ever faster.

Thus we pass from earlier notions of Olympians who in some Cartesian fashion can rationalise about the world; we pass from the veneration of selected groups of empirical or other researchers in their specialised departments. We arrive instead at a recognition that whatever information or tentative conclusions can be achieved in either of these ways depends upon institutional embodiment if it is to have a future, and upon multiple-fronted validation in society. We also need well-organised systems of manifold communication. Only thus do we pay effective heed to the deep implications of that remarkable English phrase, "making up our minds".

At this point, we may think back to the sort of comment made several times about thinkers like Dewey. Dewey saw education moving through "problem-solving" methods to the solution of several social problems, especially those implicit in a democratic society. In his time and circumstances it was not surprising that he addressed himself generally to pedagogical methods and to an audience of formal educators. In his private life, however, Dewey paid much attention to educational institutions as an apparatus for wider social, political, and economic reform, as was attested to by several of his writings on the revolutionary world in which he lived during the 1920's and 1930's.[4]

Dewey certainly survived to express impatience with those pedagogues who reduced his wider methodological aims

---

[4] See particularly *John Dewey's Impressions of Soviet Russia and the Revolutionary World*, edited by w. w. BRICKMAN (New York: Columbia University Teachers College, 1964).

to mere classroom techniques. Since the time of his formative writing, we have moved on to envisage the age-old study of mankind and man-making in a wider purview of institutional, ideological, and decision-making aspects. How, then, can we communicate it to our students and colleagues in any other guise?

Even to take the measure of comparative education as a study intended for future teachers, we are bound to recognise that all its concerns and problems, all the activities and "factors" associated with it, are diffused throughout society as a whole. Yet knowledge has grown so much that no study of any educational decision can nowadays do more than scrutinise a few facets of society as a whole. If we professionally or experimentally isolate bits, we must necessarily return them to the whole context in order to ascertain their real meaning.

Insofar as comparative education has some affinity with science and philosophy, we have recognised already that that affinity lies in three characteristics: the systematic disentangling of educational observables from a mass of generalised awareness; the systematic analysis and appraisal of education's parts or factors in relation to the whole system within which they are in ecological interaction; and the advancing of hypotheses for further scrutiny, experiment, or assessment. Thus comparative education helps to build knowledge, understanding, and skill. So much for our discipline as a means of enquiry.

The affinity which comparative education has with *applied* science in the social field (economics or forensic medicine, for example) lies in its application of that knowledge or skill to readjustments of a useful kind. First, it can show how education in its widest sense is or can be distributed between schools, industries, and other socio-political organisations—a dynamic study in times of such rapid change. Secondly, it can show how greater overall satisfaction or efficiency in some detail can be achieved. Such satisfactoriness can be helped by proposing hypotheses, or by demonstrating feasibility or priority.

Yet comparative appraisal of this kind is far more likely to be effective by relating itself to a practical series of articulated decisions in the public field of education. Such decisions might be about the structure of schools and their "flow" into later opportunity; they might concern curriculum and orientation, or deal with enrolment and retention and life-linkage of some kind. They might, on the other hand, deal with productivity and effectiveness in certain contingencies, or with the pull-and-thrust of learning, teaching, and training. Our questions might attempt to analyse training and re-training (both personal and professional) along a developmental scale. And so on. Thus comparative study—contextually undertaken and with direct practical relevance to decision—can help to provide that vital framework of decision: a public and publicised and institutionally linked *strategy of choice.*

Where does decision reside? What are the necessary antecedents? What is to be the apparatus? Each country, each problem, must clearly have its own; but the following stages of procedure are recognisable:

(a) co-ordinating information in a state of "pre-digested" relevance;
(b) the preparation of provisional expert counsel on the matter to be decided;
(c) arriving at a collective or concerted (but certainly articulated) decision in principle;
(d) programming the decision in executive terms;
(e) communicating it and securing co-operation;
(f) follow-through in existing or adapted institutions;[5]
(g) on-the-spot advice, with in-service training where appropriate;
(h) the establishment of new institutions and the training of new personnel;
(i) the securing of international contacts for co-ordinated comparative review.

---

[5] Points (c) to (f) will be considered again in relation to research procedure and research communication, pp. 150ff.

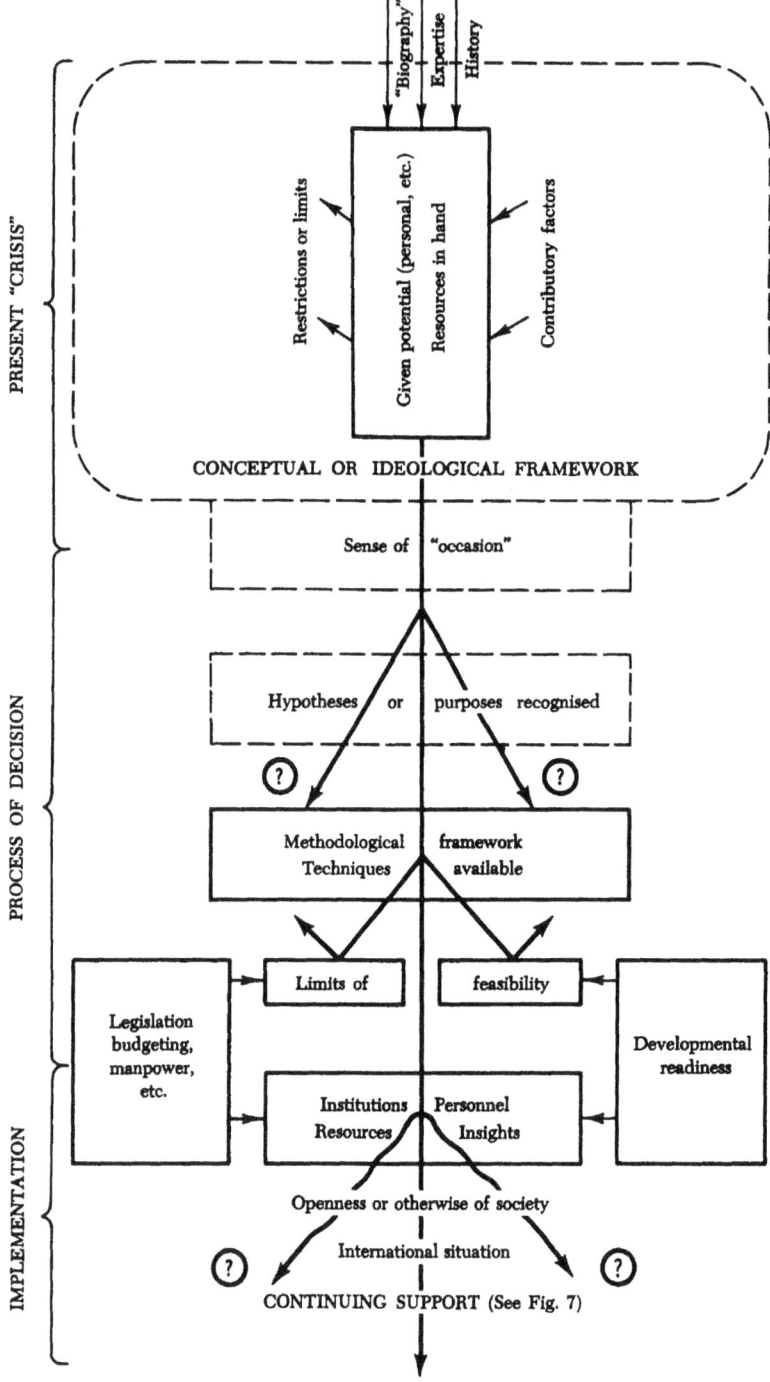

Figure 6. *Flow diagram illustrating possible factors in educational decision and growth*

Once again it is clear, and worth repeating, that the role of comparative education in this last respect is informative. A specialist in comparative education does not make the choice. Any operative choice for these days must be public and political at the same time as it is personal and professional. Not even the entire body of expert planners can, in the long run, take and justify public decision, though they are obviously of immense power in deciding economic feasibility, social consequences, and political possibility. Governments and experts often know better than the layman the present state of developmental readiness on which so much depends. That is once again what Professor Popper meant by the "logic of situations", this time at the professional level. But when all the information and all the implications of this "logic" have been fed into judgement, implementation turns on votes. Public information (or public education, if you like) is a vital factor in all democratic processes, politically speaking; it is also a vital factor in securing economic efficiency and social readiness. All these areas of public interest brings us once again to consideration of the school's part.

The *Year Book of Education* for 1965 contains excellent articles by M. J. Bowman, A. Rosier, and R. Diez-Hochleitner. These articles show the intricacy and unpredictability of relationships between educational expenditure and economic expansion, between quantitative "input" and qualitative output, or between economic growth and effective national development. No such economic growth can be expected from educational "investment" unless that process is accompanied by change throughout society. But which comes first?

Dr. A. H. Halsey of Nuffield College, Oxford, has doubted the direct efficacy of research conclusions for influencing decision. Instead of direct cause-and-effect relationships, he prefers to speak of promoting the kind of self-consciousness which makes people justify their sense of priorities. To this we might add contextual awareness, an awareness of direction and developmental readiness, and an appreciation of "the logic of situations".

All these are normally conceived of in institutional

terms. Even if that were not so, the growth of mammoth decision-taking institutions would force such recognition on us. By "decision-taking institutions" I do not refer only to such publicly sponsored activities as the research units helped or organised by the Schools Council in Britain and corresponding educational research enterprises in the United States. Even without heeding the cautionary note introduced by the writers just referred to, we are bound to wonder how much direct effect educational enquiry per se can achieve when we note that in 1966 some $22,000,000,000 were invested in general research and development in the United States alone; and of this total the United States government was responsible for more than 70 per cent. In the same year formal education in the United States as a whole cost less than $50,000,000,000. In other words, research and development expenditure outside the field of education cost almost half as much as the nation's whole scholastic commitment—instructional, institutional, research, and all the rest. By the end of 1966 the annual budget of the Ministry of Technology in Britain was some £300,000,000 (including aircraft and associated apparatus), together with another £268,000,000 on research and development. Immense though this expenditure is, it is far from being the whole of the formative investment likely to have a direct bearing on the structure of education and its orientation.

Such lavish outpouring is not confined to governments, of course. American corporations spend some twenty million dollars annually on "technological forecasting" alone. Indeed, Professor J. K. Galbraith's Reith Lectures on the B.B.C. in 1966 stressed the replacement of the free market by business planning in all countries, not least in the United States. He declared that it was illusory to think of the big enterprises' planning except in terms of comparability with government planning. Therefore there is little distinction to be made between public or private evaluation of "input" or "output" either in industry or education.

The impossibility of isolating public and private institutions altogether, and especially economic or educational investment (whether private or public), is implicitly recognised in the activities of the International Institute for Educational Planning in Paris. Since its founding in 1963, the Institute (with an American at its head) has specified as one of its central purposes that of helping nations to decide more rationally how much of their total resources might profitably be spent on education. Not only costs and financing are involved, but the different benefits or effectiveness to be expected from a variety of educational policies. Yet such information is far from being simply a specialised handout for experts. The technical advice given by the Institute has been described as inseparable from "a philosophy" to be imbibed. A major function has been to *teach;* that is, to inform and enlighten the public area of decision, and with special reference to institutional and economic decision.[6]

The Institute co-operates with interested training and research organisations throughout the world, both private and public. The inseparability of private from public interest is shown by the sponsorship of the Institute; for the I.I.E.P. was founded by UNESCO to be a semi-autonomous body, financially supported by the World Bank and the Ford Foundation, in premises provided by the French government.

If nothing more, this very proper acknowledgement of a generally broadcast teaching and information service by highly specialised technical agencies should prove to us that the orientation of comparative study and research towards practical points of public decision or educational strategy is no abandonment of the teaching role itself, towards which much attention and research have been directed in the past. It is its fulfilment in terms appropriate to to-day.

To neglect the practicalities of reform, or crises of educational priority, is in any case to neglect the real-life context of

---

[6] Compare R. DIEZ-HOCHLEITNER's article in the *World Year Book of Education* for 1965, p. 163: "Educational planning is not a magic formula that will come up with ready-made solutions. It is an instrument to channel *all* knowledge about education and related disciplines into the preparation and implementation of long-term and short-term educational development plans" (italics mine). Dr. Diez-Hochleitner's article also shows strong appreciation of the important educational and developmental role of all social institutions, old and new.

our academic enquiries and researches, and to rob them of the greater part of their meaning. Such an omission would be robbing the decision-making institutions in the various countries of the "intelligence" on which their strategy of choice must be worked out. For we cannot forget that the legislative and financing framework within which educational decision has to take place is still national, and sometimes local within the national framework. That seems likely to be the case for many years to come. In any event, the sense of significance and commitment which is so essential to the success of any educational or social programme is inevitably communicated and construed in terms of local and personal meaning.

We might be forgiven for wondering if there are not already sufficient agencies for undertaking the necessary comparative enquiries in the educational, social, and economic fields. After all, UNESCO itself has 120 member states (the number growing from time to time). It has established a number of national co-operative bodies to effect liaison between specialists at each national level. It is also linked with the United Nations system, and has ties with the food and agricultural organisations and other reconstructive enterprises. It maintains links also with the Council of Europe and other international agencies, governmental, and unofficial. It has particular ramifications with science and teaching, which now extend far beyond what governments and UNESCO themselves can officially do. It works to a budget of some fifty million dollars a year. It has both general conferences and well-organised departments. Some are concerned directly with science and scientific policy, with social sciences, and with a great variety of directly educational institutions and policy-making bodies in many countries.

UNESCO also collects and disseminates information. Its operational side is well developed and of increasing importance; and, although UNESCO can only work on the request of sovereign states, the degree of co-operation is close. Furthermore, UNESCO has been largely instrumental in indicating how educational and developmental strategy can be planned both generally and in terms of specially selected activities. It has shown, for example, how in some countries adult education will pay off better than school education at a particular time. It is aware of the wide variety of local influences on education, both positive and negative. It has wide and deep experience over a greatly varied range of educational input and outcome. In addition to this, it possesses permanent advisers and sends out specialists *ad hoc* on request.

UNESCO too, in the period since the Second World War, has exemplified the new thinking about the impact of total educational demand and educational provision on *whole societies*. Therefore it might be supposed that UNESCO is the answer to every prayer. It has certainly been the answer to many. The successes of UNESCO, and the services it continues to offer, are so manifold that no account can really do justice to their cumulative effect. In retrospect historians may declare the inception of UNESCO to be a major turning point in the use of education in the twentieth century. After all, there was real novelty in thinking of the impact of formal educational activity on whole societies.

In 1945-1946 the influence of comparative studies of education was revealed in the attempt to put order into the way educational policies were made and implemented in a variety of countries. From 1952 onwards UNESCO showed increasing concern to help developing countries to set up systems of formal education which were consonant with needs and the resources available. More recently, the indirect influence of these endeavours has been discernible in the overall development and "programming" of educational forecasting and stock-taking in a variety of industrially advanced countries. Though these countries do not seem directly to be advised by UNESCO, that influence is discernible in the tendency to take an overall view. Previous enquiries, such as Royal or Presidential Commissions, had very often dealt with one aspect only, for example primary education or some other branch; but more recently member countries have realised that not even they can really plan without overall regard to social conditions, economic resources, and the return to be expected from educational investment.

The United States is the richest country in the world and the one most elaborately served by formal institutions; but the search for national policy and national consistency in the generation since the Second World War has been quite astonishing to those able to look back to previous American assumptions about education. In fact, present American trends seem to run counter to much that is still said about American education in the textbooks of many teachers' colleges. This vast, though indirect, contribution would by itself go a long way to justify much of UNESCO's activity—even if we overlook the incalculable services offered to more obviously developing countries.

The phrase "more obviously developing" is used deliberately. All countries, as the French phrase has it, are still on the "path of development". Leaving out of account the unsolved problems of applying the logic of the Industrial Revolution to its social implementation, it has been argued (notably by Mr. Walt Rostow) that the progress of underdeveloped countries towards self-sufficiency is taken in five steps, the last of which is the point of economic take-off (including academic take-off) when they are able to maintain their future development without relying on external sources. Clearly, the United States has immense technological and scientific development; but the so-called "brain drain" tells well enough that American reliance on foreign talent presents a kind of dependence upon technological systems and university resources in other countries. The United States has not yet reached the point of self-sufficiency in this matter—and perhaps never will, because development has a way of producing further demands.

In any case, no matter what happens within a country, the happenings between countries are of such a nature as to introduce yearly new developmental problems. These are superimposed upon the indigenous problems of national systems which are closely related to a previous social structure. Thus archaisms abound. Yet countries no more readily throw off archaic contradictions than human beings throw off bad habits. UNESCO experts, or the national co-operating commissions which are in intimate touch with UNESCO, are severely restricted in the types of recommendation they can make. What may be little more than technical common sense may look like interference in the domestic affairs of a sovereign nation. At best, suggestions can only be made; countries may accept them or drop them as they fancy. Furthermore, the kinds of advice given are normally restricted to matters of organisation or technique. There are few neutral fields in which suggestions can be made without offence, for example, mathematics; but one can hardly be too explicit about social studies, language, etc.

Let us also consider the matter of educating, training, and distributing teachers. This is central to the entire business of formal education, yet it is one of the most tangled areas in the field. Teacher education and training is one of the most haphazard activities in most countries of the world. It often lacks direction; it is dependent upon the uncertainties of numbers available for training, upon the social and other structures governing the relationship of schools with one another and the outside world, and so on. It is a problem quite insoluble unless governments come to grips with a close study of educational policy and teacher supply in terms of social and economic planning for the total demands of their societies.

Once the mind ranges over the other areas of decision, the local entanglement becomes more obvious. There was a time when the main concern was to offer primary education—as it still is in many parts of the world. The more advanced countries of Western Europe tried to expand secondary education before the Second World War, and since the end of that war have tried to universalise and equalise its opportunities. Concurrently too, the development of higher and various other forms of tertiary education has been high on every national agenda. Yet every discussion of these planes of education beyond the primary stage is hot politically. Therefore, there could be no question of a body like UNESCO attempting to direct, persuade, or even adopt an avuncular role. No member state would stand for it.

It was partly for this reason that the International Institute of Educational Planning was set up in 1963; yet the Institute has been mainly concerned through its five regional centres with the more obviously underdeveloped countries. On the other hand, the kind of information or permeation of discussion by research findings to which Dr. Halsey has referred, and the results of conferences, do soak into the consciousness of those who must make decisions in individual countries. There is often a time lag between first encountering a useful idea from an alien source and assimilating it; but in a few years such ideas are very often assimilated and boasted about.

National pride and independence, however, impose limits on this process of assimilation. An illustration of this very point reveals one possible shortcoming of an organisation like UNESCO. The representatives of many newly emancipated countries in Africa and Asia are inclined to consider that the first demand on any school system must be the universal provision of a free, secular, and compulsory elementary-school opportunity. In terms of the human birthright, this point of view seems reasonable. Yet when population growth is so rapid, and economic development is so slow, and when the scanty flow of trained personnel from the schools could easily be absorbed into the elementary-school teaching profession, unpopular questions of priority are raised. It may be necessary to prefer the training and recruitment of what Sir John Sargent has called "pace-setters", or what others have named "pyramids of excellence". Alternatively, as Dr. C. E. Beeby has suggested, it might seem logical to demand quality in the teachers even at the cost of some reduction in quantity.[7] UNESCO advisers themselves indicate that in order to "prime the pump" secondary education is the greatest need in many countries. They mean particularly technical and agricultural or teacher-preparatory education at the secondary level. There is a tendency for such advice to go unheeded in member countries which are still underdeveloped, mainly for political or prestige reasons. In all fairness, too, we

---

[7] SIR JOHN SARGENT, *Society, Schools and Progress in India* (Oxford: Pergamon Press, 1967) and DR. C. E. BEEBY, *The Quality of Education in Developing Countries* (Cambridge: Harvard University Press, 1966).

should recognise that the representatives of such countries may genuinely not recognise the "logic of the situation".

Furthermore, prestige is a touchy business. Even in ostensibly neutral territory like the academic discussions of UNESCO, political and other considerations constantly come to the fore. Shortly before the time of writing, the influence of members from developing countries caused UNESCO to commit a large sum of money to the development of a journal serving primary education, though the experts are agreed that needs are far greater in the secondary and technical fields.

Another problem will be obvious to anyone who has read the official publications of UNESCO or any of its enterprises, or international publications such as those made available by the Council of Europe. International organisations receiving information from member countries are obviously precluded from editing that information or commenting upon it. Communications thus offered in the best of faith are, therefore, less respectable academically than university teachers or other independent researchers would normally accept in a non-governmental communication. Anything involving a value judgement of any kind, or a political comment, must obviously be excluded.

The implications of this kind of neutrality are greater than they seem at first. Let us suppose that a review of secondary-school leaving examinations is taking place. In any international survey of this type, the question of providing alternative ways to the university, or alternative subjects which might be offered at university entrance level, is bound to seem radical to some, though the language used may seem conservative to others. Then any survey of social change accompanying alterations in the composition of a school population, or in the structure of schools accommodating boys and girls between fifteen and eighteen (for example), may again be construed as a reformative enquiry likely to stir up partisan or sectarian resistance somewhere. Therefore, international organisations tend to avoid such issues, though by any truly neutral criterion these are the very topics which most urgently demand academic research and social surveys of a contextual kind. They are precisely the sort of study that the UNESCO example has commended to member countries ever since its foundation.

Of course, such enquiries are greatly needed *within* member countries. This remark particularly applies to federally organised or decentralised countries such as the United Kingdom or the United States.[8] What is true in any relationships between the fifty American states will in the long run be partially true for any review of educational systems within the member states of the European Economic Community, though with more complications. Patterns of school change in Western Europe show fairly consistent response to international interdependence and to the consequences of change in the occupational and technological structure of the countries concerned. How then can any review of examinations, school curricula, or the supply of teachers be relevant either nationally or internationally if that survey confines itself to the already existing school provision instead of paying attention to that likely to be required by the exigencies of to-morrow?

Thus it seems clear that within each national system of education and research there should be a built-in apparatus for continuous "examination of conscience", for determining obsolescence and insuring replacement of the obsolete, and also for international comparison of notes—all transcending the official limitations imposed by the institutional structure of an organisation like UNESCO or the Council of Europe's Education Division. That does not mean failure to co-operate with these exceptionally valuable organisations; but it does mean insuring independent research and review, perhaps in concert with the officers and conferences of these organisations.

---

[8] See, for example, FRANCIS KEPPEL, *The Necessary Revolution in American Education* (New York: Harper & Row, 1966), p. 68. "Educational needs can no longer be, if they ever could have been, considered apart from society's other needs—or from politics". Keppel's entire book, and indeed his recommendations over a number of years, argue the need for a total policy-making review of American commitment to education— in social, political, and international perspective.

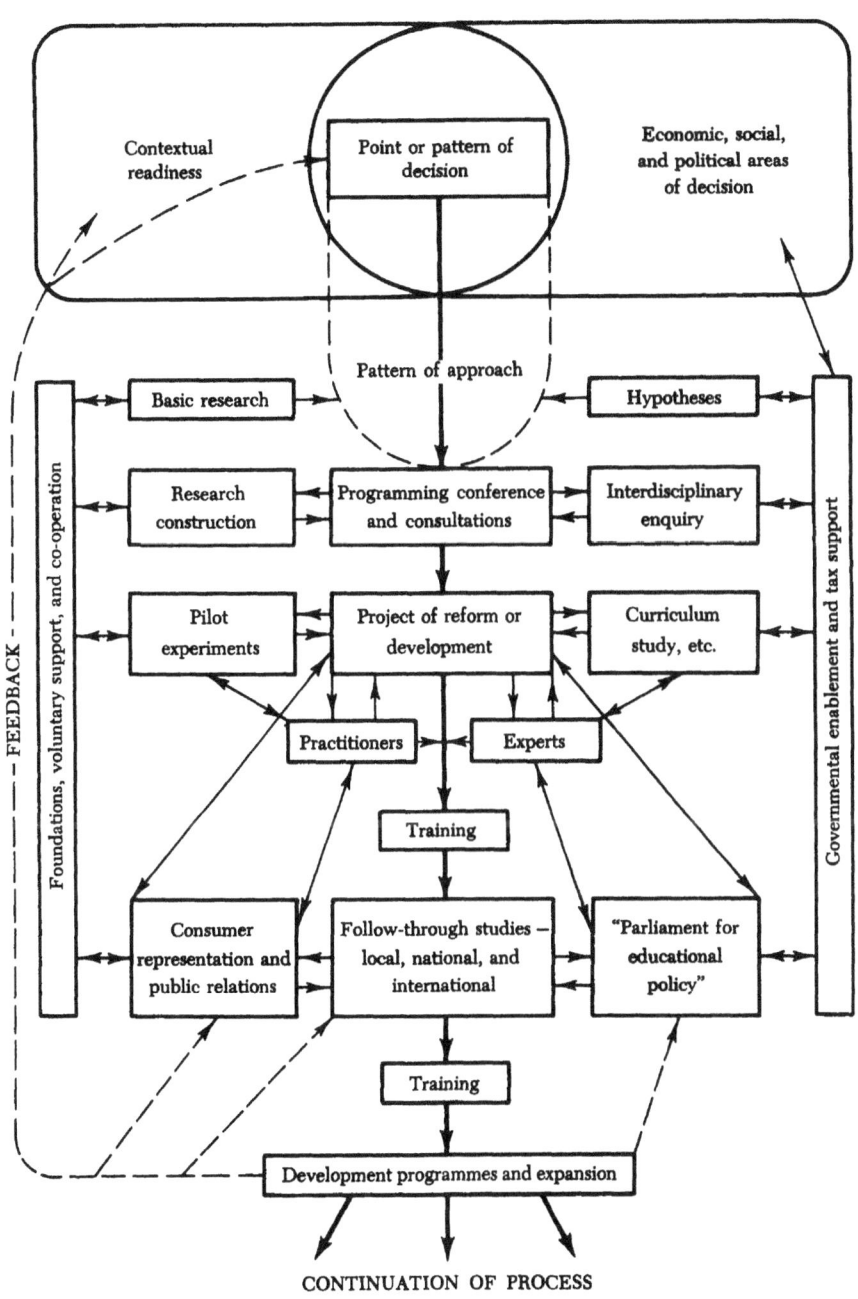

*Figure 7. Continuing structure of decision, implementation and review (see Figure 6)*

Indeed, the international organisations welcome such a relationship. They are not blind to the limitations which their own constitutions impose on them. Thus the strategy of choice could continue to be national (perhaps even local in some instances), while the supply of information and enlightenment for that strategy could be internationally appropriate. Even if UNESCO or any other international organisation were perfect, local re-interpretation and follow-through would be necessary. To demand it is no condemnation of international co-operation but a tribute to its relevance in every local setting.

There is, of course, no question at this stage of envisaging any supranational *authority*. UNESCO and other bodies are at most partners in an enterprise invited by governments. They do not even act as experts or as programmers and managers on behalf of governments. The very correct neutrality of such internationally co-operating bodies prevents them from enjoying any of the licence which a national body of reviewers or advisers might possess in its own confines. The latter kind of review body, therefore, has more opportunities for outspokenness and directness of approach for advice.

National bodies for research or advice such as the Schools Council in the British Isles, or policy-exploring bodies such as those recommended by Mr. Keppel for the United States, are likely to be needed more and more. Indeed, over and above the purposeful enquiries commissioned by such organisations, there seems to be scope for one or more comparative review bodies with a more roving commission. By this I mean something licensed like the King's jester of old to offer comment in season and out of season. It might show real imagination in a more off-beat way than bodies more respectably commissioned for specific, official enquiries within the national framework.

As we have repeatedly seen in this book and still more in this chapter, the need for continuously creative decision-making with full alertness to the significance of international change logically calls for something of this kind. It is true that there are formal departments of comparative education in many universities, and departments with some comparative interest in an increasing number of others. It is also true that there are departments of economic and social study which to some extent review related phenomena and problems, though these need to be more closely linked with our special research into society's educational functions and formal education in particular. Also, such studies as telecommunication in some of the newer universities suggest implications for such a comparative review, since they survey the social and human aspects of communications in addition to the technical requirements.

We recognise too that there are journals in which ideas can be communicated. There are also Comparative Education Societies in North America, in Japan, and in Europe. Yet when all this is added up, it still looks like an ill-assorted scatter of specialists. Our comparative education experts are mainly preoccupied with teaching or teachers' researches; our sociologists and economists need hardly communicate with the latter except on an occasional or personal basis; the telecommunications people have much to cope with in an industry which is doubling its size every six years, without spilling over into other experts' territories; the higher education experts have special problems of increasing numbers, of expanding knowledge, and of articulation with schools and industries. Who is charged with surveying the articulation of educational problems as a whole in relation to the immense changes overtaking any one country and its international connections?

Of course, more research must be continuously undertaken in all the fields of enquiry. Yet all this new information, and all that already lying around unabsorbed without being systematised into significance, clearly needs piecing together. Communications do not happen; they must be organised. Not merely must the existing information be made to tally wherever possible; it is equally important that omissions be accounted for and articulation secured. Some overall *parliament for educational policy* needs to be given corporate existence and continuous life and apparatus. Optimally, it could be independent of the government, having multiple bases in the several universities or educational research centres. Inevitably, its flow of information and contacts for discussion would transcend the limitations of university departments or the present working divisions between university and research specialisms. The area of concern would undoubtedly have to extend far beyond the limitations of the formal instructional apparatus and its personnel.

There are important questions here for any consideration of governmental responsibilities in the modern world; but the problems raised are especially pertinent to the administration and re-orientation of education. Let us look at questions of general concern in modern administration, and then consider the case of education separately. The first thing to note is that technological and international complications nowadays mean that hardly any Minister or Cabinet (though charged with decisive powers for which they are answerable to "the people") knows the assigned sphere of decision except in strong outlines. The detailed knowledge necessary is supplied in various ways: by junior Ministers and political secretaries; by *ad hoc* committees and commissions; and by the permanent secretariat or civil service. Sometimes Ministers also have a private office to "do the quarrying" for them. But when everything is added up, the assembling and pre-digestion of material tends to fall more and more on what are often called "mandarins" (the career civil servants and administrators).

Now it is notorious that good civil servants do not precipitate themselves into decisions. That is not their job, after all. The higher the repute of the civil service or other branch of administration, the more likely it is that its members will be ultra-correct and cautious, and will, furthermore, represent in their own experience the "best" schools and universities as well as the "respectable" academic interests of their distant youth. Lord Snow has said that the time-scale of applied science is ten times faster than that of politics. Yet the time-scale of political decision may be much faster than that of top-level administrative commitment.

Much reliance, therefore, is nowadays placed upon commissions, which can give *ad hoc* and often relatively independent advice. (It depends upon their composition and the terms of reference.) But the work of commissions can go awry; their parturition may deliver a "ridiculous mouse" or a "child born out of time". Even if they are very much to the point, their reports have a way of being half-implemented or simply filed away through no fault of the commission. Events often overtake the necessarily slow deliberation of *ad hoc* commissions. In any case, commissions often survive their usefulness.

To solve some of these problems, semi-permanent commissions or corporations are sometimes set up; sometimes they are called "Authorities". It is easy to think of several in the United States, in Britain, and in Western Europe. To avoid recriminations, none will be named; but it is obvious that the best of these "authorities" have proved valuable in rescuing the decision-making and development required for enormous constructive enterprises from the realm of political caprice and the administrative dead hand.

Roads, communications, nuclear energy, waterways, and natural resources are spheres in which they have been tried. Specialist scientists and developers, technologists and businessmen, are all engaged together with politicians and other "representatives of the people". Some specialists are seconded; others are career men and women. It is extremely important to make sure of having career specialists in this new, *accelerated* form of information-gathering, co-ordinating, and direction-discerning organisation.

This kind of body need have no standard shape or commitment. The British Broadcasting Corporation may or may not serve as a further model in Britain; and the existing "authorities" in the United States and continental Europe may be only the forerunners of a multiplicity of new types. The point at issue is that a new type of inter-Ministerial, interdepartmental, interregional, and sometimes international body can at times serve with functional efficiency and executive speed the direction-finding requirements of parliaments and technical specialists and of "the people" themselves. *Ad hoc* short-term commissions (often localised too) can no longer do that. Their terms of reference may preclude the offering of large-scale advice. At times whole governmental administrations fail to do so, with all their resources. Even when they could, they are sometimes inhibited by major overall considerations of strategy or international policy.

Education is rather a special case for a national "authority" in the sense used above. Although it brings into play the political, economic, social, regional, and personal vagaries which make decision-making such a labyrinth, it is in some ways a more hopeful sphere than other socio-political areas. There is immense goodwill on the part of administrators (no matter how blinkered or misguided). Most people are finally convinced that "the best for all" is the best for their own children in the long run. Parents, children, and other consumers of education have strong feelings, and a strong commitment too to the shaping of legislation and its implementation. Confidence can be gained and field enquiries reinforced by the manifold gathering-up and communication of information which has been envisaged in this chapter.

Indeed, without some such device all education is a flop, and most social reform also. Nonpartnership becomes a serious social and political problem in these days of more recognisable (or more widely claimed) equality. Once upon a time subservience and hierarchies took care of such things as public order, public cleanliness, public morality, etc. Nowadays we know that if such desiderata are attainable they can be secured only by having an orderly, clean, and moral public. But how?

On the face of things, it looks as though most of our countries, both internally and internationally, have suitable devices already for "incorporating the people" into the totality of public life. Much apparent education and opinion-reckoning, however, is more ceremonial than effective. We are sophisticated enough to see that much "conversation" is more ceremonial in character than true intercourse. Because of our past failures, and also because society is changing so fast along a multiplicity of fronts, we need more than ever to establish devices which will facilitate and require truly *constituent conversation.*

As part of its very nature, education needs to have its

institutions and personnel purposefully shaped and kept up to the mark, so as to serve the "public intelligence" and direction-finding needs enumerated in this chapter and diagrammatically represented in Figure 4, p. 31. It almost certainly means a polynucleated "parliament for educational policy" of an unprecedented kind at each national level, if only to gather up what is already known or surmised, and to assess direction and developmental readiness. Obviously, such a body could work with a corresponding international forum for educational policy recommendations, outside but alongside government commitment.

Some countries may believe that they have taken steps to establish something of the kind, at least in embryonic form. Almost without exception, however, such plans are laid on the basis of ancient concepts within the framework of existing institutions. Or the field may be restricted—perhaps to curricular change, for example. Far more alertness is needed, with special reference to comparative indications of what might be needed from well-attested sources beyond those at present contributing information or ideas. Educational "strategy", when looked at critically, seems all too often a petty business of local and contemporary *tactics*. Major international and technological influences as well as international changes tend to be ignored.

Any modern structure of well-informed decision must depend upon the official establishment of proper institutions for the nation-wide review of existing shortcomings, for providing hypotheses of research, for financing and directing socio-educational research, and not least for the developmental and internationally contextual appraisal of whatever is nationally decided. This kind of developmental appraisal in internationally relevant terms necessitates a stronger, wider, and more systematised *comparative* ingredient than has hitherto been acknowledged in any formal way.

The point may be illustrated with many examples; but let us take the familiar instance of the "brain drain". To any student of comparative education it is fairly obvious that one reason why European (and particularly British) scholars are attracted to institutions in the United States has nothing directly to do with money, or even with career prospects as such. The hierarchical and pyramidal form of British universities continues to restrict the research interests and academic growth of many brilliant people in the middle age range of an academic career, bringing developmental possibilities to an untimely end because of the narrowness of many departmental heads. By contrast, it has been obvious for a long time that university organisational patterns in the American universities allow or even encourage the lateral development of interests so as to include new "subjects", new applications, new contacts in the same or other universities, etc. The plateau of achievement and of personal status is thus much higher for the average person working in a good American university. Of course, this brings financial and promotional advantages; but careful enquiry on the ground in British and American universities by anyone with comparative insights leaves no doubt (without further research) about what many young academics find professionally irksome. What is true within any one British university may equally apply to inter-university relationships, and to the isolation of universities from other enterprises acquiring ever increasing prestige in a modern state.

This kind of insight, though offered frequently enough in the correspondence columns of leading newspapers, appears to be frequently left out of official review-body considerations. Yet without this kind of subtlety, which careful comparative study has been fostering over a long period, the best official estimates of the likely consequences of many educational policies are likely to be what the cynics have begun to call "guesstimates". Such sneers appear to be justified by the abortiveness of much otherwise well-conceived planning.

To summarise the general drift of this chapter, I might simply repeat that decision-making and "taking thought" no longer depend upon the mere serving up of information at various points of the compass. If research communications and learned advice are to be effective in the modern world, there must be a proper apparatus for multidimensional communication leading directly to all those centres concerned with planning and decision, including the political field. Not even the best of national data banks, however, or the best information-retrieval system can suffice alone. To be of any use at all, local and national decisions about education must be relevant in world terms. This presupposes a strong comparative ingredient. It also means that such apparatus must have strong international connections. But so far from being a solemn senate sitting at the right hand of government, it would be better for any body charged with such review responsibilities to have a more widely roving licence of the kind suggested above. We are not thinking of a legislating body. Nor can there be any question of mathematically predictable concepts or hypotheses to be followed by a firmly validated proof. If any such proof were achievable to-day, it might be irrelevant to-morrow.

In any case, which body or bodies so far have been charged with the duty of co-ordinating the existing comparative evidence? This, though directly relevant to education, is equally relevant to all studies affecting the economic and social future of any nation. What body can reliably report on the existing educational planning and experiments of other countries? At any rate, what body independent enough of legislative pressure and financial consideration gives advice which includes value judgement or "politics" of the type excluded by the constitutions of UNESCO, the Council of Europe, and similar bodies?

As soon as any innovation is proposed in a school system, diehards generally complain that the change is made without experiment or "research". In these days, there has usually been plenty of both in other countries, but in comparable circumstances. The lack is of communication, not relevant experiment. Whose responsibility is it to report on and assess the educational reactions of other countries to the approach of automation or of atomic power? Many governmental departments and many academic interests have fingers in these pies. So they should have. But the institutional framework is lacking to make sure that their various interests and contributions are gathered up *structurally and institutionally* for the making of modern decisions in education. Certainly no structured basis exists for continuous review of the ever accelerating obsolescence of all decisions—especially in the powerful educational activity which is shaping the future.

In considering these requirements, we can hardly forget that to-morrow's world will be one of accelerated change and ever deeper interaction. What was said in the previous chapter about preparation for overseas service and other technical co-operation also applies equally (or more so) to future international encounter in the commerce and scientific relationships of advanced countries. The "Six" of the European Economic Community, the "Seven" of the European Free Trade Association, and the specialised agencies of Euratom or the Coal and Steel Authority are but a few familiar examples heralding a type of international conversation which will be no less important than old-style diplomacy. It may be more important, for it may exemplify the only way in which co-operation and *knowledge* can be furthered. Certainly, thought is already being carefully given to the education and training of what the French call *les responsables de demain*—the experts and administrators responsible for guiding the international development of to-morrow.

Therefore, it is imperative to provide not only for organisms through which co-operation and interaction can take place, but also for the initial training and lifelong re-training of such strategically placed experts. They cannot work within the framework of special interests sufficient for yesterday, because a quite different complexion and structure of decision-making is to be expected. "To determine the nature of the *process* of decision is in part to determine the nature of the policies themselves", says Keppel.[9] Undoubtedly, failure on our part to make preparation for constituent and complementary information-gathering (or use of it) will hamstring all attempts to take our civilisation to the next phase of the dialogue—of multifaceted discussion.

We should not be so naïve as to suppose that, if govern-

---

[9] *Ibid.*, p. 56.

mental bodies and universities fail to devote attention to such communication needs, a merely negative handicap will hamper future-building. The Biblical story of the seven devils may be remembered here. Education is already the biggest single industry of many countries; and if governmental agencies do not assume responsibility for this new sphere of big business, private enterprise will. It has already done so in notable ways: first in the textbook business, and more recently in all the realms of audiovisual aid, programming, and "help yourself". The "education industry" can be so described in a new sense these days—particularly in countries with a relatively decentralised diffusion of responsibility and a growing dearth of really powerful and far-sighted teachers, or at any rate a dearth of opportunities for such remaining teachers to shape the perspectives and contacts of formal education.

What is at issue now is not the possible usurpation by *states* of educational responsibilities which in former times might have been left to parents, communities, and churches; it is whether the public agencies of education can measure up to the planning and perspective-formation which is the very nature of modern *business*. And modern business does not merely have ideas; it has organisation and trained personnel—for the purposes of business in the narrower sense of that word. The real business of mankind, however, is making man. Only the "first round" of the Industrial Revolution thought it was enough to make *things* and so make money; the second and more important phase, now beginning, is the application of that capital equipment and skill to the release and use of human energies for the benefit and sanity of all mankind to-day and to-morrow.

To forswear responsibility for the guidance, training, and institution-building now demanded is to abnegate the central responsibility of any civilisation. We have more problems and vastly more uncertainties than any of our predecessors; but then we have resources, knowledge, and self-understanding far beyond their imagination. Why not then move with courage and public committedness to a task which others readily take up for profit or partisan interest? Though the central interest of this book is in education, the kinds of study, training, and institution-building envisaged here are already acknowledged to be a proper part of the study of management and of public administration. Why not then take them one stage further, to ensure a deliberate link between formal education, policy-making, and the other decisions of government?[10] Nothing very revolutionary is entailed by this recognition. Professor C. von Weizsäcker of Heidelberg University has already pointed out that roughly half the academic labour force of Western Germany is directly employed by the government. Of the others, a quarter are doctors or dentists, whose incomes are decisively influenced by governmental health policy though they are not directly employed by the state. In the United States, what would happen to private industry and public schools if governmental policy and finance for the space race were suddenly withdrawn? We need more frankness in facing the public realities of "private enterprise" in relation to collective policy decisions.

Let us consider some additional reasons why it is necessary to take that further step of preparing people and institutions deliberately for continuous decision-making and decision-implementation. Since medieval times (or before) we have been familiar with the idea that authority was unitary, visibly institutionalised in state or church, and permanent. Authority was very often juridical; that is, one simply had to know what had been determined and who had determined it. However, the rise of Protestantism, the spread of self-government, and the ever wider extension of peculiar specialisms during the Industrial Revolution all familiarised the idea that "truth" and "understanding" had to be built up from many separate insights. But each insight had its own *corporate* "authority" or its special-

---

[10] Some of these possibilities were reviewed in an unpublished dissertation presented in 1955, and later in my *Education and Social Change* (Oxford: Pergamon Press, 1966), especially Chapters III and IV. Since the present chapter was first written, supporting ideas have been noted in FRANCIS KEPPEL's *The Necessary Revolution in American Education*, especially pp. 67 and 121–123, notably in a reference to Dean Sizer's comments.

ised and incontrovertible skills or knowledge. Such areas of organised specialisation have in the modern world been invested further with the aura of scientific authority or business efficiency. Useful though corporate specialisation is for some purposes, those purposes could still remain blinkered and *functionally isolated*.

The big change introduced by the modern world has come because (in addition to juridical authority and the "authority" of expertise) the relevance and perhaps "authority" of *varied public experience* is acknowledged—in all kinds of decision-making. In religious or political opinion, in choice of marriage partners, in consumer preference, and so on, we do not question the need to contribute individual or group views to a pluralistic and (so to speak) *existential* awareness guiding decisions in the body politic.

There is little new in this generalised statement about change in the nature and abode of political authority. But what of its consequences for the channels of educational communication and the structure of decision-making? Looking back, we see what kind of institutional pattern was favoured by authoritarian kings or unquestioned churches. More recently we note that the preoccupation of science, technology, and business with efficiency and impersonal expertise has produced its own routines and its own hierarchy of communication and authority. But the pluralistic and existential shift just referred to clearly necessitates a different structure for communication, a different structure for decision-shaping, and systematic re-education for all those engaged in the process—whether they are experts or "lay" participants. That means a new institutional framework and a new conceptual framework with a "comparative" or constituent approach as well.

Otherwise, the businessmen, the administrators, and all the existing pressure groups which owe their origin to other purposes will continue to follow habitual practices and habitual relationships. They will almost automatically transfer noneducational routines to the business of educational development and educational-political decision. Who, then, has effective responsibility for choice, or room for it? It is clear that choices must be made with fully and continuously formed "intelligence", by people with proper training for it, and through a publicly responsible apparatus devised for the type of decision-making needed in our times. Any comparative study of education at work clearly necessitates a commitment to the construction of that apparatus, and its maintenance.

In this last connection we may recall Professor Galbraith's contention: that the forms of political government or of the business boardroom are frequently little more than ceremonial. People "go through the actions" though the decisions are all too often pre-determined by "experts" above them whose choice has been influenced by apparent functional need or business advantage—certainly by very different considerations from those supposed to operate. Institutional arrangements not only teach people skills and attitudes; unfortunately they often relegate policy-decisions to a kind of managerially conditioned response.

Everything talked about in this chapter, then, requires to be "institutionalised", not only in terms of using existing opportunities and institutions but also in terms of devising new ones. "Authority" in policy decisions affecting education is widely diffused (if we pay any heed to the contentions of this book). Therefore, a quite different mode of "institutional language" and "institutional debate and experiment" is called for in order to foster the necessary flexibility for continuous decision and review.

The pedestrian pedagogues of the old regime were trapped in their own system. The administrators and policy-makers are now becoming trapped in theirs, partly because of the very success of our school systems in making the world of to-day. But what we are thinking about is taking decisions for the world of to-morrow. In default of reorganisation on our part those decisions may be made by others who are not in our cage.

*six*

# A PROGRESSION

# OF

# COMPARATIVE

# STUDY

The re-orientation of comparative studies in relation to education has been fairly fully dealt with. In Chapter Three an outline of the shape of studies was given. In Chapter Four attention was given not only to the shape or structure of studies but also to their increasing commitment in the world of activity and decision outside. A brief account has also been given of the historical development of comparative education as an academic study. The previous chapter was concerned with the necessity for having a comparative review institutionally built into all decision-making processes which affect education, and into procedures for securing implementation of educational policies. Now we can address ourselves to the relatively simple task of outlining a progressive study of comparative education proper.

It will do no harm to recall the framework of our previous analysis. Comparative education was seen to proceed through the following stages:

(a) information (of a provisionally analytical kind), with special reference to the global idiom and growth-climax of one or more cultural patterns alien to the observer;
(b) educational questioning and analysis of a more transcendent kind, dealing generically with "problems" occurring cross-culturally (but all needing to be pieced back into context in order to make real sense);
(c) more exact identification of a problem for research, or for enquiry into the developmental dynamic of the problem thus examined;
(d) research programmes of a concerted or reformative kind;
(e) active commitment to public service, with its implications for training or re-training, and for the establishment of institutions of communication and decision.

In reviewing these considerations we take account of the changed role of comparative education—intellectually, in time, and in its milieu or context.

Let us think a little further about the last point, the present context of our study. It is especially relevant to do so because the place which comparative education occupies as an intellectual exercise is not the only thing that has altered with the passing of time and the very changed role which education plays in the modern world. In considering comparative education not too long ago, one would think only of teachers. Even if thinking of teachers now, one has to bear in mind not only the imparting of information during a period of initial preparation but also the probability of in-service review, and the pursuit of some intellectual or pedagogical interests far beyond the level once considered appropriate to intending teachers. Thus it is not simply a matter of a curricular subject for the first teacher's certificate (or for a first degree in the United States which mainly serves pedagogical purposes). All countries are now providing a more advanced first qualification for the abler teachers—degrees in place of certificates, and a higher intellectual content in any case.

Moreover, the teacher is seldom thought of only as part of school personnel. The teacher is much involved in the activities of the modern world. Its challenge increasingly requires a comparative attitude of mind and the continuous appraisal by international comparison of whatever is done domestically. The growth of a consumer world and a sense of growing civic responsibility make teachers answerable not only to their local authorities or to their own parent-teacher association but also to a much wider public. Their consciences are more sensitive too.

A richer and more mature approach to comparative studies of education is also demanded by alterations in the composition of those who come to study it. Throughout the world there is constant concern to induce married women and those who have graduated in non-pedagogical subjects to take up teaching. Moreover, the idea of international service has induced many would-be teachers to spend one or more years abroad in low-income countries during the early part of their lives. Such people returning to teaching want something rather different from the fare of the undergraduate or teacher-in-training once familiar. The general increase in sophistication, both social and intellectual, demands much more of any comparative study of education than would once have sufficed. The inclusion in comparative study of sociologists, area study experts, and similar well-qualified people also enhances the considerations just outlined.

Therefore, even the supposedly simple level of "information" can no longer be confined to the kind of introduction which once had to pass muster. The kind of programme enrichment for teachers recommended by Dr. J. B. Conant (for example) necessitates something much more substantial. Parents and electors also need something more thoroughly informative, and more dynamically analytical. What was said earlier when we were reviewing the possibility that research or economic input can enhance both educational and economic output also needs to be thought about here. The amelioration of education and the raising of economic and social levels can be achieved only if there is a substantial and sustained change of heart on the part of the general population. Therefore, in considering who is likely to need the information and insights of comparative education, we have also to bear in mind the enquirer who is a layman (pedagogically speaking) but is certainly no novice when it comes to making mature decisions about education (civically or parentally speaking). Finally, in any review of education and the role of schools, we need to take account of the ascending level of general education on the part of the public at large. Thus it is as true of comparative education as of any other educational aspect that information and discussion in the world of to-day are a vastly more complicated affair than before the Second World War, let alone the beginning of this century.

Let us now proceed to consider possible bases. For a good beginning to the systematic comparative study of education at least four distinct approaches are recognisable. The first of these could be from some type of mainly sociological study. Included in this general area or perspective we could reckon historical, geographical, or related studies. In some ways distinct, but still germane, is the background of those familiar with the wider public issues of education's social and economic responsibilites.

A second group of enquirers are those coming from a generalised "area study" of some kind. Such people may be specialists in the overall study of a particular area (for example, South America, Islamic studies, or South-East Asia). Among this general group we may consider those who have undertaken voluntary service overseas, as in the Peace Corps, or who have served on a technological mission of some kind or in foreign commerce.

A third group includes those who have specialised in the language or literature of a particular culture, without paying much attention to its educational complex, and perhaps without much acquaintance with its socio-political development. Many such students are first-rate material for a class in comparative education, though they still need a rather preliminary type of presentation.

A fourth group are those who approach the comparative study of education on the basis of a formal study of education itself, for example in teacher preparation. Here we also recognise the experienced teacher who suddenly realises the need for a comparative awareness. The administrator familiar with only one system's intricacies on an empirical basis, and without sociological preparation, can perhaps be placed here also.

For all these people it is evidently necessary to provide a complementary basis of comparative study dealing with education to-day in various ways, but always against a background of *almost total change*. That is to say, from the very beginning the idea of educational *relativity* must be communicated. The items of any country's educational practices or tactics relate to the total pattern of its cultural "self" at this particular moment in time. That present-day "self" (in order to be identified at all) must be considered along some sort of developmental scale or scale of change—even in relation to its own progression from its past into the future. Hence at this early stage of information there is no question of pure description. The information given has hypotheses and a sense of direction. Moreover, the national or cultural identity whose wholeness is communicated to students as a kind of language of ideas and framework for decision is revealed in its relativity by the very fact that some comparative study is begun. The hypothesis is made that other people's experiences or insights are relevant to ourselves. These points have been made before; but they are worth repeating in order to underline the fact that even elementary awareness includes some hypothesis or assumptions about the procedural pattern for study.

The very fact that a group of students contains people from such a variety of academic backgrounds and personal or professional experiences may be a huge advantage. It reveals from the start the complementary nature of our methods of enquiry. At the same time there is no point in assuming that even a relatively advanced body of students can get by without a really thoroughgoing acquaintance with the cultural pattern of one or more countries. If nothing else, this procedure will act as a focus of enquiry. It will bring into play the insights and information introduced by the student body, and will certainly bring home the basic truth that no "problems", methods, or identifiable data can be truly discerned before there is thorough familiarity with the dynamic context in which they occur. This challenges as well as clarifies the conceptual framework within which the observer takes note of his neighbour's behaviour and proceeds to analyse it.

Moreover, there are other reasons for choosing *countries* as a beginning of comparative acquaintance. Obviously, governments are charged with educational legislation and its implementation. National or local budgets are very much official matters determining the amount of money available for school buildings and programmes, and for the payment of teachers and others concerned with education. Countries often prescribe items of the curriculum, and teachers' qualifications. Custom and legislation place the schools in a particular hierarchical order. Admission from one school to another, and to universities or careers, depends upon qualifications which are often officially legislated. How can one discuss educational problems or phenomena except against this strongly controlling national background? Nowadays control is not only legal and financial, but often directional as well. Educational orientation and priorities are an integral part of much government planning.

Even if that were not so, there are many forceful constituents of any educational complex which must be borne in mind. Already referred to is the subtle containment of the "cultural envelope". This obviously includes the national sense of identity, the language or languages spoken within a country or other cultural unit, together with all the religious, literary, and other reminders of a national "self". Though we often think of these separate ingredients or totalities as permanent, they have markedly recurrent climaxes. Yet even these climaxes are often identified nationally, and sometimes bring out to a remarkable degree the sense of national identity. These are but a few of the reasons why it is important, if not essential, to begin with a strong awareness of a cultural idiom and its powerful communications.

The emergence of new nations and the rise to power of hitherto depressed cultural units have enhanced rather than diminished the kind of popular force more readily recognisable in old-style nationalism. Many a new nation has had to found its nationhood on a somewhat synthetic self-portrayal displayed in every school. A national language is given pre-eminence. Indeed, sometimes a foreign language (such as English) has been adopted to impose a common idiom of communication on regions which obtained their independence without a commonly accepted language of their own. Norms of achievement are set; examination and promotion patterns are distinguished; and new kinds of technological or political salvation are sketched, to be worshipped by the young under the co-ordinated guidance of their teachers. All such countries have severe problems. Any solution demands the scrupulous use of every scrap of resources. Among these the existing schools are the most precious. Sometimes the indigenous culture can be relied on to give strength; but sometimes this is repudiated in favour of an abject copy of Western-type schools and Western-type nationalism. In any case, expansion or enrichment takes place within a national framework, even though many elements are now recognised to be internationally transcendent in these days of ever closer communication and interdependence.

Books written to satisfy this preliminary stage include Vernon Mallinson's *An Introduction to the Study of Comparative Education* and my *Other Schools and Ours*. Both of these books take pains to communicate the concept of "a culture" and of cultural idioms. They show how cultural idioms are associated with particular national territories or regions. Mallinson draws special attention to the concept of "national character" and of public ideals. Fallacious though these concepts may be in terms of genetics or biology, they may be truly powerful educational influences. They have led conquering armies on the rampage; in more peaceful ways they have preserved Judaism and the

Armenian and Greek identities. The revival of Denmark after the Napoleonic War and the elaboration of the co-operative movement and other forms of collective enterprise in Denmark from about 1870 onwards both owe very much to the essential idea of "Danishness". Yet he would be a very bold man who presumed to prove that the Danes were a nation in any other than a cultural or educational sense. This is but one series of examples of how particular elements can be cemented together in a sense of national or cultural identity.

At this stage it may be important to show how particular patterns of belief, of public administration, or of co-operation between individuals and groups may run together. Without claiming scientific exactness of any kind, one may point out that Roman Catholic countries (especially those where the Jesuits achieved great power at various times) are characterised for the most part by centralised patterns of administration. Linked with these characteristics is regard for one central source of "authority", not only in religious matters but also in intellectual enlightenment. Such countries often have a strong regard for excellence as selected, rehearsed, and vindicated by exhaustive examination systems. By contrast, countries marked by Protestantism (especially of a dissenting kind) are more inclined to believe in a varied and empirically based approach to the solution of both material and secular problems. Here some authorities like to draw an ancient lineage. They point to the settlements of the Angles, Saxons, and Jutes in the forest, each self-sufficient though vaguely in contact with the nearest kin; they then draw conclusions from this information for a development of self-determination in the Americas or in the American classroom to-day. If any such lineage exists, it is likely to be a matter of social inheritance and of direct teaching in the schools, chapels, or in the way of organising life; in other words, it is once again a matter of cultural co-ordination and inheritance of institutions rather than of genes. For the student of comparative education it is interesting to note that cultural institutions and habits are grouped in patterns small and large.

The trend towards larger units of industry and commerce since the Industrial Revolution has not altogether impaired the pre-existing patterns. It has sometimes reinforced them, notably in Japan. In trying to establish a trend towards deliberate public change, nations have hitherto relied largely on existing practices and values. The tendency to assess any particular national requirement on the basis of an overall national housekeeping plan (which has been noted several times here) served in the early post-1945 period to entrench some of these attitudes. On the other hand, the increasing co-operation between nations (as in the Western European Economic Community, in the Colombo plan, and in other regional co-operation schemes) has made it easier than it used to be to secure close co-operation between nations for educational projects of an international kind and for the re-appraisal of indigenous standards, even though the several nations retain responsibility for their own affairs.

Once this kind of initial survey has been undertaken, the student is ready for the higher levels of analytical enquiry already sketched in the early part of this book. If it seems appropriate to stay within the field of studying intensively one or more particular national cultures and national patterns of decision-making, the student is well served by books in the *Society, Schools and Progress* series. More than twenty separate volumes have been devised; each provides an inside view of a particular country in some detail, with reasonable penetration of its social problems and administrative patterns, in full process of adjusting national self-identification to the transcendent needs of the modern world. These books treat most of the major factors and considerations of comparative education within a relatively uniform sequence to facilitate cross-cultural comparisons.

As already noted, books published by O.E.C.D. have reviewed the affairs of European countries and the United States with the same kind of conspectus, but with a more strongly economic basis. From the end of 1966 onwards, the International Institute of Educational Planning in Paris has produced short monographs on similar trends and problems, mainly within a national framework and on the Continent of Africa. Some of the earliest volumes deal with Nigeria, Uganda, Tanzania, and similar countries. The United States Office of Education has done a similar service for a number of countries, but with a more strongly pedagogical ingredient. Some of those volumes are very valuable indeed, notably the studies published in great variety and depth about the educational and planning characteristics of the U.S.S.R. and other Eastern European countries. On the basis of books like these, following the overview provided by books mentioned earlier, a whole year's work can be profitably undertaken with students at a mature level. Seminars and discussions will doubtless reveal similarities and recurring problems.

Bit by bit the characteristic features of particular school systems or of general educational patterns become distinguishable. It is easy to recognise the extreme form of the European idiom as exemplified by France. We can see how this pattern has been profoundly influential in neighbouring European countries. Sometimes the similarity is due to direct copying of France; sometimes it is due to parallel influences (such as those of the Jesuit pattern of organising schools). South America was also conspicuously influenced. The Arab countries, too, followed the French example to a large extent, not always by imperial conquest but because of direct cultural borrowing.

Again one can see the North American idiom growing: exemplified in the United States, very similar in Canada, and again followed to an increasing degree in the English-speaking Dominions of the British Commonwealth. Decentralisation, self-sufficiency, egalitarianism, a preference for the empirical and local approach, a strong regard for the family and the child— all these things markedly cohere as educational and social influences. The very problems posed by latter-day trends towards greater participation by central government (extreme in New Zealand and the Australian states) are again worth looking at in what we may call their family connections.

Alternatively, one might pay close heed to education and politico-economic planning as exemplified in the U.S.S.R. In the period between 1868 and 1940, one might have said similar things about Japan's educational system; but though the Japanese example was before Russian eyes, the Soviet idiom was essentially different. The Chinese example is more to the point to-day, and attention may be drawn to the valuable survey provided by Dean Chiu-Sam Tsang in his book *Society, Schools and Progress in China* (1967).

In all such studies the familiar "factors" referred to by Dr. Hans and Dr. Schneider are fully revealed—but in a rather different way from the masterpieces of those two great scholars in comparative education. The emphasis is off determinism or "driving forces"; the several discrete influences are not seen separately; nor are the factors seen only historically and retrospectively. Instead they are envisaged as part of stock-taking and decision-making for the future. In other words, each case study nationally surveyed or individually reviewed is referred back to the complex national system and to the analytical framework within which each of the authors of the books mentioned has begun his survey.

At this point it begins to be possible to go more fully into some of the particular factors or recurring *problems*. Some of these may be called recurring or perpetual. Among these are the problems of poverty, of color; of town versus country; of women's education; of urbanisation and related influences. Philosophical and ideological problems are just as important to-day as the ethnological or linguistic data given prominence in some older writing on comparative education.

Equally vital are some of the basic school questions: "Who is to be educated?" "How long?" or simply "How?" Very important and transcendent problems to-day are those of the supply of schools, teachers, higher education, technological education, and the whole relationship of learning to teaching. So are the problems of relating school structure and curricula to social and technological change. It would be presumptuous to claim solutions to such perennial questions and problems. Yet some orientation to question-*asking* can be given, and at least some report can be offered of solutions proposed by others in their school systems. This was precisely my intention in writing

*World Perspectives in Education*. Some family likeness between the problems can be recognised in this way. Such vague resemblances (allowing each individual his identity) are more appropriate and more reliable than the alleged identity which some scholars affect to discern. Another book in the same general category is *Contemporary Education* (1956) by Cramer and Browne. Both these books provide a conspectus of several problems in a form appropriate to students and teachers or administrators at the second level of enquiry. There is a recognisable distinctiveness in the recurrent problem studied; but problems are seen (a) in context, and (b) in their interrelationships or linkage.

Individual problems or linked problems of a particular kind can be reviewed at a later stage, perhaps as a study for the second half of a second year of comparative study. Among these one may deal with a particular type of education, as in the collection of essays edited by me on *Communist Education* (1963), or *Access to Higher Education* edited by Dr. Frank Bowles (1963). The Robbins Report on *Higher Education* published in Britain in 1963 also contained in one of its volumes an excellent account of patterns of higher education in a variety of countries. The Council of Europe has published several volumes on *Common Trends and Problems* and *Teacher Education* in European countries.

At this level even the more mature student with a strong political background or with technological interests can benefit by detailed American surveys such as those by Nicholas de Witt on *Soviet Education and Professional Manpower* (1965), and A. G. Korol's earlier but excellent work on *Soviet Education for Science and Technology*. Dr. Nicholas Hans has two scholarly and revealing books on Communist education—almost exclusively in the Soviet Union. The American publishers of the journal *Soviet Education* also provide some analytical rather than descriptive information of a contemporary though not unrelated kind. In the same general category of intensive study of educational types one may mention the excellent book by Dr.

C. E. Beeby, *The Quality of Education in Developing Countries*, which is mainly concerned with providing effective teachers.

At this second level of problem enquiry, the *World Year Book of Education* annually provides an introductory editorial on a theme chosen for the year, and a series of essays written by experts (usually in relation to their own countries) on the one general theme. For example, the 1959 volume was on "Higher Education"; 1960 was on "Mass Media"; 1961 was on "Concepts of Excellence"; and the following year dealt with the provision actually made for the gifted child. In 1963 the main theme was "The Education of Teachers"; in 1964, "Education and International Life"; in 1965, "The Education Explosion"; and in 1966, "Relationships between Church and State in Education". Thus there is now an abundance of material on the problems of education, treated either in monograph form or in the form of essays related to national contexts, but in the encyclopaedic envelope of a yearbook's co-ordinated survey.

Of course, it is not suggested that comparative surveys of this kind are divorced from the sociological work of researchers surveying the specialized influence of particular social factors within their own countries. A great deal of excellent work of this kind is done and must continue to be provided, not only for the enrichment of understanding within countries but also in order to provide well-attested material for international surveys. On the other hand, we have already pointed to the piecemeal nature of much sociological enquiry. Even if the sociological overview which Professor Shils was mentioned as recommending is established, there still arises the problem of international comparisons.

For this reason it is important to work closely with those university and other departments which are concerned with large-scale developmental studies—economic and sociological surveys of an international kind, and similarly related studies. At no time must the suggestion be allowed that comparative education, even within these specialised fields, is a self-contained unit. Indeed, for the study of such influences as the expansion of the school population staying on beyond the age of compulsion, and problems of a consequential nature, it is obvious that more and more interdependence of study must be recognised. These are transcendent, not local phenomena, even though they have local peculiarities from which we can never escape.

Nevertheless, at what was earlier called the third level of research or enquiry, it is possible to conduct not only the detailed researches of academics which lead to university theses and dissertations, but also the kind of reform-oriented analysis which increasingly appears to be important in current decision internationally. Topical research fields include the following: economic resources; problems of technical training and/or general education; problems of higher education; "permanent education"; the recruitment, education, and roles of teachers; the structure and relationships of secondary schools and their curricula; methods of recruitment and transfer in secondary education; trends in occupational structure and change; the consequences of automation and similar innovations; youth and its relationships; the use of new materials, new media, and new forms of presentation or programming.

Questions of internationally comparable attainment in mathematics, in the sciences, or in language teaching are relevant here too. At this level much value is added by internationally collected and evaluated material. Empirical researches are of great importance. Though in the past many of them have been written in peculiarly national form—so much so that they may be internationally unintelligible—it is now becoming easier to re-use the same empirical data stored as a result of relevant studies in order to secure a further yield from it. Now it is also clear that more use may be made of the same or similar methods to obtain, systematise, and analyse new material which may be relevant to educational improvement or policy decisions in comparable countries. Similarly, insights derived from particular disciplines for the improvement of education may lead to the discovery of further sources of information or new testing methods. Indeed, the extent to which empirical material is reported in *Comparative Education* and the *Comparative*

*Education Review* for international communication would have been surprising a few years ago. In any case, all this reporting of material and research techniques is useful in helping to check existing conclusions, and suggest new interpretations and hypotheses. It all adds up to a rich foundation for whatever independent research projects we have in mind.

A great deal of material, some stored on tape and computerised for various purposes, is available for a second working-over in comparative studies directly related to education. It will be years before the material acquired by the International Evaluation of Educational Attainment (IEA) yields all its significance. The same is true of economic and sociological or planning studies amassed in several centres. If permanent research or conference centres for comparative education could be set up, as described earlier, continuous "clearing-house" or appraisal exercises would provide a wealth of information.

While thinking purposefully about our own lines of enquiry, it will be helpful to relate our research intentions to the procedural outline given in Chapter Five, and again to the logical progression sketched on the first page of this chapter. Not only will practical hints be provided to facilitate our task; the logical and professional connection will also be shown between academic research, our own recommendations, and other people's practical or political choice.

The suggestion frequently made in this book that we should always begin by taking careful stock of our setting and its developmental stage has enhanced value here. We recognise our own and other people's involvement in patterns of awareness and perception, prompting us to focus attention on particular points of interest in such a way that we see a "problem". However, it is obvious that there may be no problem at all if other people have already provided a solution or nearly so, or have seen more clearly than we what is involved in the situation which disconcerts us. Thus, commonsense requires an informative study of what is already known. Unfortunately commonsense is not always heeded, especially when it comes to crossing disciplinary frontiers. Therefore, a reminder to become thoroughly familiar with what is already published is not simply tedious pedantry. The development of modern bibliographical services in many American universities and a few of the more alert ones in Britain shows how much material has been steadily overlooked. Furthermore, the growth and intricacy of modern data banks require assiduous attention on our part, and indeed reliance on people who can provide that type of information as a basis for our study far more skilfully than we have ever managed in the past.

Then if we know our setting factually, conceptually, and with some provisional ideas about direction and method, we can go on to think more earnestly about the important matter of our developmental stage. Where will our enquiry take us? Where will its outcome take other people? Is there any future for what conclusions we all reach? To see this avenue of questions in some sort of perspective, it may be helpful to deal with them first generally and then in some detail.

If we are well informed about the proposed field of enquiry, we shall doubtless hope that our project's outcome will take us to a "next point" on some developmental scale. Then the general questions to be answered include the following:

(a) Will the next stage be a continuation of the present?
(b) Will a new hypothesis or new data be required?
(c) Or a new-style implementation?
(d) Will a new institutional shape of some sort be needed?
(e) How will our outcome or proposals be articulated with others in the same general context?
(f) What seems likely to be the general overall consequence?

As we thus generally survey the proposed field of enquiry, gradually focussing and narrowing our immediate concern, we shall almost certainly find ourselves repeating the same or similar questions in relation to one particular existing institution (in the broad sense) or one particular crisis of decision on our part—linked inescapably with other people's decisions. For the speed and scope of change alone mean that decisions are being *continuously* taken on matters that once seemed obvious or settled.

So while we work out our special plan of campaign and our detailed methods, tests, and possible outcomes, we remain acutely conscious of what might be called a *frontier of interaction*. That frontier probably delimits not so much the settled area of some other discipline, all nicely tamed and clarified, but a real terra incognita. That is another reason why research work (and teaching, for that matter) is often best done if it includes at least a well recognised area of "block interaction". The time has passed when everything had to be or could be dealt with separately at all times. Therefore, if other disciplines or other colleagues can be induced to work over related themes in one general area of common concern, all gain by it. That is true for reasons of knowledge and technique alone; but it is doubly true when we see that whatever solutions we arrive at will have to be fed back into what seems to be the existing or continuing institutional situation. I mean into the same school system or the prevailing climate of opinion, and so on, even if what we propose or discover seems to be a corrective. The same sort of dilemma is found also if change is obviously going on, because it may not be what we envisaged or helpful to our purposes.

Therefore, all enquiries, to be profitable, need to take account of existing institutions which may restrict the outcome in some way, or which may shift in directions we may not have ascertained, or which, in any case, may need to be assisted in their further evolution by the developmental insights we offer. This observation seems valid no matter how much we shun the role of reformer, because otherwise our observation is misdirected in being applied to a world of unreality. For academic accuracy no less than for topical relevance we need to "go along with" a directional and purposeful survey of what follows from our observations and reports. In other words, we are intellectually committed, whether or not we feel so morally and emotionally. However, the possibility of making that kind of distinction has been severely questioned since the first decisions about the atomic bomb. Can professional integrity these days dispense with the idea of public service and committedness that has always been implicit in the time-honoured professions? Whatever we feel about that, there is no escaping from the fact that research in comparative education by its very nature is directed towards a public area of engagement and decision, which shapes the field and detail of its interests, and its methods as well. The same point was illustrated in Figure 5.

Sometimes new or unsuspected problems are revealed by this kind of research. For example, lack of articulation between the parts of a national school system may be thrown into prominence, with their consequences of "alienation" or discontinuity and related educational problems. In developing countries the adoption of an alien school system throws such disjointedness into bold relief. Yet even well-advanced countries may have much to learn from the international sharing or pooling of research findings or insights. The educational problems of the socially handicapped, or of youth and other sections of the population who seem isolated either temporarily or altogether, are instances that spring to the mind. Moreover, one best becomes aware of trends by the international sharing of comparable research findings, methods, and recommendations. Even an apparently unique enquiry of a distinctly narrow kind (like the international study of mathematics achievement) can become a rich mine of important ideas and lines of enquiry.

At this research level of comparative study, we are on the planes variously described earlier as the third and fourth levels—depending on whether it is mainly detailed academic research, or decision-oriented communications into the international field. In normal British and American practice, this level of enquiry would almost certainly be undertaken at the graduate stage (perhaps as a doctoral thesis). It comes after considerable preparation not only in the introductory subject matter and into the insights of problem analysis, but also into the appropriate techniques to be used.

The fact that real research comes third in the logical scale of progression in comparative education must not be taken as indicating a belief that no formal learning needs to be added between the second and third stages specified for comparative education as such. It may be important to add somewhere some further sociological, economic, or methodological advice. Techniques appropriate to special interests may have to be studied. Certainly that is true if any original research is to be undertaken.

On the other hand, it is conceivable that the third *type* of enquiry, at a not very advanced level, could well be used as a "project method" for learning the significance of comparative education, especially in the case of teachers in training. Where term papers are to be written or individual assignments are found profitable, this method is particularly helpful; though it cannot be expected that the "researchers" will add very much fresh knowledge. However, they may well do so. Moreover, teachers employed about their daily business are often able to develop their own sense of a comparative attitude and gather professional insights at the same time by re-appraising comparatively their own daily work and its problems. This may not add much to the scholarship of comparative education; but it certainly adds a great deal to the professional and personal participation of the teachers concerned. If in-service conferences and conversations can be promoted to enrich teachers' insights, the kind of continuous review which nations need at the top level will be maintained at those intermediate and lower levels which are integral to the health and communication processes of a democracy. The humane and participant value of activities of this kind is far greater at this range of professional responsibility than any intrinsic value it may have as a contribution to scholarship. But it is a kind of activity without which all the amassing of research information undertaken by scholars will fail to communicate effectively.

Some of the outstanding problems seem to be in great need of contributions from this level of enquiry. The total body of problems in any one national situation may be unique, and enmeshed within each national situation in a kind of indissoluble unity affecting every one of its parts. Nevertheless, the elements may well be distinguishable for study. Effective solutions or diagnoses in any case require the involvement of solution-seekers in their context. That context may be the real-life factor making or marring solutions we propose. Problems of comprehensive schooling or "middle school" are not matters only for the realm of ideas. They obviously depend very much on the realities of here and now. "Backyard" insight and solutions may be more to the point than those loftily handed down from the study or the Ministry.

In any case, the articulation of problems with one another is best seen through the daily involvement of the day-to-day practitioner. Questions about the effective selection process for schools, or for jobs, or about the means of communication, all turn upon actual practices and structures which may not have been evaluated by remote researchers. They may not even have been spelled out; and if they have, there may still be no procedural guidance and no proper conceptual analysis. For example, how do we measure the significance of a system to its members? How do we measure people's involvement? How do we assess the relative status of institutions for various purposes? How do we distinguish intellectually between education as an inner personal and social experience, and education as a public system or apparatus used by persons for career purposes of their own? If we do, how do we appraise the difference?

What is legally defined and formally available may be unofficially put to very different uses and subjected to unimagined strains. The methods and techniques of personal use, and the idiosyncracies of interchange between a nation's educational elements, are only partly explored. As Professor Basil Bernstein has pointed out, the English educational system has many formal faults of selection-and-rejection; but one of its most serious problems in actual practice is that so many people leave school because they have made up their minds that they are "out of it". The Newsom Report (*Half Our Future*) revealed the half-suspected prevalence of severe social handicaps discouraging schools in many cities and industrial areas, though optimists thought them a thing of the past. "Operation Headstart" was devised to remedy a similar pattern of disadvantage in the United States. Here is a kind of revelation to which local and on-the-ground enquiry by practitioners can helpfully contribute. There is plenty of scope here for comparative enquiry as well as for locally based sociological research, provided that the relevance of it for comparative study is frankly recognised, and the communications system referred to in the previous chapter is properly implemented.

Indeed some such communication, of a strongly comparative dimension, is essential to the success of any research, no matter whether undertaken at the simple level of practical innovation or whether part of a long-term, top-level enquiry. Otherwise it is impossible, or at least difficult, to make sure what is due to schooling or to the experiment itself, and what is perhaps due to contextual or topical influences lying outside the experimenter's hypothesis. Apart from the practical advantage of communicating already existing information, this is a supreme research contribution of comparative insight.

Of course, within each national boundary there are now remarkable constellations of research sponsorship which help communication and the establishment of "bridges". Thus, within any one national boundary, researchers and experimenters now move beyond their domestic terrain. The increase in official sponsorship for co-ordinating schemes of this kind, and for communication, has in recent decades surpassed all previous bounds. For example, in the United States the disbursement of the United States Office of Education on research grew from nothing in 1955 to 101 million dollars in 1966.[1] In England and Wales the National Foundation for Educational Research (sponsored then, for the most part, by the local education authorities) not long ago conducted the greater part of educational research. Recently the annual budget was more than £138,000. The Schools Council sponsored by the Department of Education and Science (as the former Ministry of Education is now called)

---

[1] F. KEPPEL, *The Necessary Revolution in American Education*, p. 123.

now sustains the greater part of research into the curriculum, examinations, and educational development and innovation in Britain. Existing foundations and societies and the research and in-service enquiries encouraged and financed by Local Education Authorities are thus given a greater sense of direction and cohesion, though much remains to be done in this respect. Perhaps it will be imparted in Britain by the new "Planning Branch" of the Department of Education and Science.

However, the major directional flow of educational development and of structural evolution is not to be ascertained within one country's perspective alone. Important though it is to establish the major constellations of interest and politically practicable priorities, some of the problems now occurring in one country can have much light thrown on them by information from other, outside sources. The information given is sometimes valuable on its own account. Useful experiments can be reported. Of greater long-term importance is the indication of major directional trends, new structural possibilities, the challenging use of manpower and resources in new patterns of redeployment for educational use, unsuspected factors for success and motivation, and, indeed, the general formulation and examination of questions which may not even have struck the observers in their domestic setting.

It is this kind of encounter which makes much supposed "strategy of educational choice" in one particular country look like short-term tactical adjustment to a clutter of indigenous preoccupations, which prevent educational thinkers from seeing the wood for the trees. Without lending credence to deterministic theories, one can certainly surmise the existence of underlying trends or possible indications for the future (as far as we know it). At the very least, these provoke hypotheses for further enquiries and allow us to eliminate some of our own superstitions.

The extent to which superstitions prevail is nearly incredible. We need not go into any contemporary examples. We might remind ourselves of a few from the past; that is more convenient and less embarrassing. It appears from the writings of Galsworthy that women must ideally stay at home as elegant foils for menfolk (all of whom seem to belong to the favoured middle class). Similarly, women in most countries of the world stay at home and have children, one after another. Are some of our superstitions of this order, or do they go even further into paradox? "Who ever heard of a woman cook?" asked Plato.

Unsuspected superstition may persist in such matters as the apparently automatic justification for raising the school-leaving age to sixteen or eighteen in Europe—if that means that everyone must have an extended general education according to the prevalent interpretation of what general education means. The entire question of relating general education to real-life involvement is of major importance now that thoughts for the fifteen- to eighteen-year-olds must concern not only the small minority once given the thoroughgoing academic treatment familiar in the French *lycée* or the German *Gymnasium*, but must include perhaps 70 or 80 per cent of the total population within a few years to come, and perhaps 100 per cent after that. When boys and girls are marrying much earlier, and, in any case, are bored with school as they know it, and eager to get out into the life of adult experience, is there not something to be learned from comparing the experiments of other countries such as the United States, the U.S.S.R., and Denmark, with regard to boys and girls of this age?

Has enough thought been given to questions of relating the provision made in secondary schools (especially upper secondary schools) to the state of developmental readiness in the country or region concerned? No matter how much we commit ourselves to equality, we may have to come to some hard thinking about whether or not equality always means identity. In any case, any review of the technological or social engagement of young people (or adults) raises at least two other questions in articulation with it: the question of further education during what is sometimes called the "continuation education" phase, or follow-up at a later period in life; and the whole question of the impact of already perceptible ripples of automation on education and society.

In Western countries where industrialisation is fairly well developed, there are also important studies to be made on a comparative basis of some of the unprecedented influences of rapid mobility, and of urbanisation's new pattern as seen either in the outlying suburbs of major conurbations or in cities transformed by new industries, such as Toulouse and Grenoble. Many of the parents there are themselves young, while both parents and children have a reasonable prospect of entering an industrial organisation closely linked with some new technology or its corrollaries.

Other transcendent social and educational changes must be envisaged in consequence of international co-operation or co-ordination, as seen in the Western European union, or in looser federations of states for mutual benefit. This is the sort of realm in which information from other countries can really be used *comparatively*, not simply as a matter of report but as compelling us to compare influences and considerations in a way that induces reflection. It compels us to identify what may be truly relevant or of prior importance. Many of our supposed priorities are really reflections of our own social punctilio or mythology.

For worthwhile educational decision, the major consideration is whether you drift or take conscious heed and benefit of insight. It may occasionally be necessary to do violence to one's susceptibilities. This was noted earlier in the matter of providing universal elementary education. The question is whether to spread it thin on the ground in poor countries. Some highly reputable thinkers greatly prefer the immediate establishment of a few well-appointed "pace-setters" or "centres of excellence" which can act as a sort of educational leaven to facilitate the later establishment of primary and general education on a more satisfactory basis. But must this be the choice? Can new devices produce a better solution? Again, if we are to have universal literacy, is it to be "for its own sake"? Or is it to lead to the *effective* literacy which derives from the continuing use of books and other materials to improve the lot of human beings who have learned a simple reading technique? And may not adult education, community education, and political education be of paramount importance to countries with a very low income? Otherwise, dissatisfaction may make literacy unaided by other educational prospects simply an aggravation of hopeless discontent.

Unwelcome questioning of this kind is to be faced in most countries, even those best endowed. Parents in every country (and statesmen in response to them) are emotionally involved in yesterday's ambitions for their children. Schools offering the most abstract and "gentlemanly" fare are those which attract most support in most countries. One complicating factor to-day is that an almost endless vista of abstract and unrelated offerings is placed before young people conscious of their own physical and social powers, and very often full of concrete interests which modern society does not allow them to explore. Throughout the world, school-leavers often wonder what school was all about. If the ingredients of the familiar curriculum *did* suffice hitherto for literary and mathematical training or pre-technological competence, could the success of 10 or 25 per cent of the children justify the boredom and disaffection of all the rest?

If such curricular elements must be there, may they not possibly be communicable in other ways? Perhaps at different times, or in a different procedural order? Does the examination structure and method serve the needs for which it is allegedly intended? How much of the journey through school is real discovery, true problem-solving, and an approach to understanding? How much is really a matter of historical legacy, and local archaism? Many possible answers to these problems can be offered in a given national context; but it is far more likely that international comparisons in areas which manifestly affect the whole world as never before may give some signposts across a wilderness that lacks any well-tried path.

Even in the well-tried realm of school, with the well-recognised phenomenon of the teacher, that phenomenon is in a very equivocal position when we consider the learning process to-day. Can we go on getting good teachers in to-day's job structure? How do they keep up to the mark? Who else teaches besides the teacher? Are teachers deployed to best advantage? Is their labour really a help to learning? Could the work be better programmed? Could it be better supplemented? Is there any chance of a more effective follow-up in adult life? Can we predict or surmise future roles, and make educational adjustments to the prospect before us? So far schools have been certain of themselves and of what to do; but as I have stated elsewhere, the entire shift has now begun from teaching to learning, and from handing on certainties to exploring the unknown.[2]

The general climate of uncertainty may be a Socratic beginning of wisdom. Yet such initiation to wisdom needs Socratic midwifery. Information about experimental work, or about systematic research, in these days requires the intelligent and co-operative participation of teachers and students on all fronts—and also of administrators. We cannot bear too much freedom. In any case, freedom is not isolation. Systematic and institutionalised communication as referred to in this book is needed for the diffusion of innovation, and for incorporating all responsible citizens and professions in the innovatory process. The constituent parts of modern knowledge are widely diffused, and inevitably require some co-ordinating process. The uncertain meaning of much research news (at least with reference to its social implications) necessarily demands a provisional and comparative attitude of mind. Education is now being charged, as no instrument has been charged before, with the task of shaping the future—at a time of greater uncertainty about the terms of reference and about the instrumentation of that purpose. Comparative studies are the very essence of the continuing enquiry that modern education is seen to be, with no false divisions between research and experiment, between teacher and learner. Only in this way can a continuous decision-making process be established. For in educational decisions relevant to

---

[2] This is a central theme of my *Education and Social Change*.

the modern world no one stands alone, and no one alone can take thought for himself, much less the others.

Thus we see that even in the apparently straightforward pursuit of progression in comparative study (rather than direct action) we inevitably find the researcher's enquiry pushing sideways into the collateral interests of development, trial, and dissemination of awareness. Proposals for research are likely to run alongside projects of development, for good ideas demand not only communication but experimental essay. Some institutional apparatus for experimental action therefore seems as necessary as apparatus for communication.

On the personal side, we need "translators" of research into practical propositions, and the educational equivalent of production engineers. Otherwise, it is impossible to think consecutively of structure, practice, flow, and output—though education as a conscious endeavour is really about these things. We take their articulation for granted; though obviously it is impossible to undertake observations and produce hypotheses only on the national or international level. Local centres of innovation and development need to be established and charged continuously with responsibility for aiding new growth.

Some Communist countries employ large bodies of "scientific research workers", some of whom are roughly comparable with doctoral students and research assistants in non-Communist countries. Others roughly correspond to fully professional members of research units or a scientific or economic branch of the government service. Socialist and capitalist governments increasingly resemble each other in the systematic employment and training of such workers. That is an admirable trend; but it would be a pity if the net result were the withdrawal of all these talented people out of the daily foreground in which so many pupils, parents, teachers, and local administrators continuously make their experiments and derive potentially enlightening insights.

Thus we see that whereas ancient forms of instruction were once concerned with one-way knowledge, a more recent trend has been to popularise involvement in shaping intellectual processes or sensibilities. The need for the future may well be to discover new techniques and formulae for effectiveness-in-action of a constructive or reconstructive kind.

In actual fact, so far only the Communist or Socialist systems of education have moved effectively in this direction on a large scale, though democratic ideals as expressed in English-speaking countries have long looked forward to such changes of educational emphasis. We see them firmly enough in Robert Owen, in John Dewey and his successors, in much postwar legislation in Britain and the United States, and especially in the aspiration to establish a "Great Society". For education to be viable at all, it must have a future in recognisable outcomes. Some of these seem relatively certain, and can be prepared for by curricular adaptation or structural reforms at least when these are modified to become flexible and welcoming instead of cocksure and restrictive.

The big educational and political questions of the future turn on the consequences of uncertainty and growth, on nuances and relativity which demand of every participant a state of *readiness for creativity*—intellectually and in terms of skill and opportunity. It would be foolish in a single book to look for more than a series of pointers, with perhaps a more complete coverage of one particular aspect. The aspect dealt with here seems germane to many contingent interests. It is the development, evolution, and systematic use of comparative studies as an aid to educational clarity, honesty, usefulness, and decision.

To this end I have endeavoured to link the justification of comparative studies with what is known about how we observe and think. Then an attempt was made to show how comparative studies can be an aid to honest enquiry, while admitting that such enquiry is nearly always motivated and made relevant by humane commitment. The topic for Chapter Five was how to give that commitment an effective future in a world which has not so far devised an apparatus of communication and partnership for the making and implementation of decisions about educational and cultural change. Finally, we came to see how, starting from what we have already developed in comparative studies of education (mainly for teachers in the first place), we can go on to link research interests with practical day-to-day crises of decision.

In the long run we can be successful only if we recognise that these decisions are now continuous at every level, and resolve to place the entire school process at the centre of this activity—itself creative, and responsive to all the creativity around it.

*selected bibliography*

This bibliography in no way claims completeness. It is intended to serve the progression of comparative study already outlined in Chapter Six, and to indicate the existence of additional resources. In some cases the latter consist of authoritative books. Sometimes it is more a matter of referring to representative works in a rapidly expanding field. Elsewhere it seems preferable to point to bibliographies. Occasionally we can do no more than indicate some frontiers of common interest with comparative education. Along them we can see purposeful studies of social and technological change, of economic dependence on educational reform, of new methods of social and educational analysis. Thus the present bibliography differs somewhat in content and orientation from other book lists less concerned with the developmental aspects of comparative education. A full reckoning of conventional resources in this field can be made by consulting the various source books named, according to the reader's consciousness of need.

However, as the output of books relevant to studies of educational decision and development is already vast and is growing yearly, some omissions seem inevitable. Within a year or two it will be necessary to seek a supplementary list—not only because new books will have appeared, but because new interests or emphases will make old books less directly relevant and perhaps inadequate. That is one reason why such invaluable "milestone" books as I. L. Kandel's *Studies in Comparative Education* (1933) are omitted. The present work is not a history of comparative education, but a contemporary analysis of its relevance to urgent decisions. The nearest we come to the old requirement of pedagogical courses in comparative education is in making sure that teachers too are participants in educational decision. Therefore even teachers' and students' books included here will be of the more analytical kind which emphasize developmental aspects of comparative study. In fact, the very shift in comparative education itself requires a bibliography with a new complexion. The grading of the bibliographical stages outlined below will enable any reader to find works appropriate to his own or his students' readiness.

1. SIMPLE COMPARISONS OF "CULTURES" AND EDUCATIONAL CONTEXTS (BY COUNTRIES)

KING, E. J. *Other Schools and Ours.* 3rd edition. New York: Holt, Rinehart and Winston, 1967.
MALLINSON, V. *An Introduction to the Study of Comparative Education.* London: Heinemann, 1957; revised edition, 1967.

2. GENERAL FACTORS INFLUENCING STABILITY OR CHANGE

HANS, N. *Comparative Education.* London: Routledge and Kegan Paul, 1950.
SCHNEIDER, F. *Triebkräfte der Pädagogik der Völker.* Salzburg: Otto Muller Verlag, 1947.

More recent are:

CAPELLE, J. *L'École de demain reste à faire.* Paris: Presses Universitaires Françaises, 1966. Translated into English as *Tomorrow's Education—The French Experience.* Oxford and New York: Pergamon Press, 1967.
KING, E. J. *Education and Social Change.* Oxford and New York: Pergamon Press, 1966.

3. MORE DETAILED STUDIES OF PARTICULAR CONTEXTS UNDERGOING CHANGE

BARON, G. *Society, Schools and Progress in England.* Oxford and New York: Pergamon Press, 1966.
DIXON, C. W. *Society, Schools and Progress in Scandinavia.* Oxford and New York: Pergamon Press, 1965.

GRANT, N. *Soviet Education*. London: Penguin Books, 1964.
———. *Society, Schools and Progress in Eastern Europe*. Oxford and New York: Pergamon Press, 1967.
HALLS, W. D. *Society, Schools and Progress in France*. Oxford and New York: Pergamon Press, 1966.
KAZAMIAS, A. M. *Education and the Quest for Modernity in Turkey*. London: Allen and Unwin, 1966.
KING, E. J. *Society, Schools and Progress in the U.S.A.* Oxford and New York: Pergamon Press, 1965.
———, ed. *Communist Education*. London and Indianapolis: Methuen, Bobbs-Merrill, 1963.
LEWIS, L. J. *Society, Schools and Progress in Nigeria*. Oxford and New York: Pergamon Press, 1965.
SARGENT, SIR JOHN. *Society, Schools and Progress in India*. London and New York: Pergamon Press, 1967.
TSANG, CHIU-SAM. *Society, Schools and Progress in China*. Oxford and New York: Pergamon Press, 1967.

Some twenty parallel studies in the "Society, Schools and Progress" series are in preparation, including volumes on Australia, Canada, Germany, Israel, Japan, the Arab world, Turkey, the U.S.S.R., and the West Indies.

A comparable series of monographs, but with more emphasis on economic and manpower considerations than on education, has been published by the Organisation for Economic Co-operation and Development since 1962. O.E.C.D. publications have the virtue and the vice of representing an official point of view, on the whole. Surveys of Sweden, the United States, Greece, Italy, and Austria have appeared, in addition to more general O.E.C.D. publications, such as *Curriculum Improvement and Educational Development* (1966).

Whereas O.E.C.D. surveys relate to industrially advanced countries, publications by the International Institute for Educational Planning in Paris deal predominantly with low-income countries. In 1966 and 1967 some valuable monographs appeared on a number of African countries or regions.

Some governments publish in English accounts of their own school systems, either in general or as studies of particular problems or reforms. Notable are a number of short volumes on the Dutch school system (1960), on Sweden, Norway, and Denmark. Though "official", these surveys are often admirably objective, and have the advantage of being associated with studies of social and economic developments. Since the end of World War II and the growth of international agencies such as the Council of Europe, several governments have submitted praiseworthy reports to those agencies as a basis for international appraisal and discussion.

A variation on this practice is the publication by the United States Office of Education of monographs on educational structure and trends in a number of politically significant countries, often in low-income areas or within a communist sphere of influence. Many are richly informative, but mainly on scholastic details and statistics rather than the total educational complex.

Thus it is clear from the bibliography alone that comparative studies of particular countries or contexts are now much more analytical and dynamic than "descriptive". Even when the intention is to provide readers with a rounded picture of a country or cultural context as a whole, consideration of the impact of change and challenge introduces analytical criteria. Indeed, some volumes dealing with only one country do not by themselves present a complete picture of its school system but concentrate instead on questions of world-wide importance which have recently become critical there. Among these we may instance Rector Capelle's book mentioned above, and Francis Keppel's *The Necessary Revolution in American Education* (New York: Harper and Row, 1966). In any case, consciousness of world-wide, recurring questions or problems makes recent writers in comparative education handle even local decisions in international perspective. This tendency enables readers to move more readily and significantly from one-country studies to the more transcendent examination of particular problems. Indeed, without that preparatory "siting in context" some alleged studies of prematurely diagnosed "problems" become so theoretical as to be fictional.

4. RECURRING PROBLEMS

*General surveys*

CRAMER, J. F., and G. S. BROWNE. *Contemporary Education*. New York: Harcourt, Brace and World, 1966.

KING, E. J. *World Perspectives in Education*. London and Indianapolis: Methuen, Bobbs-Merrill, 1965.

———, ed. *Communist Education*. London and Indianapolis: Methuen, Bobbs-Merrill, 1963.

MALLINSON, V. *An Introduction to the Study of Comparative Education*. London and New York: Heinemann, Macmillan, 1967.

*Specific questions*

BEEBY, C. E. *The Quality of Education in Developing Countries*. Cambridge, Mass.: Harvard University Press, 1966.

BEREDAY, G. Z. F., and J. A. LAUWERYS, eds. *World Year Book of Education*. London and New York: Evans Brothers, Harcourt, Brace and World, 1957–1966. Each annual issue deals with a particular theme or problem, of which examples are given below:

        1957—Education and philosophy
        1959—Higher education
        1960—Mass media
        1961—Concepts of excellence
        1962—The gifted child
        1963—The education of teachers
        1964—Education and international life
        1965—The education explosion
        1966—Church and state in education

The editorial introduction in each case gives a comparative survey of the topics covered for that year, since individual contributions generally relate to one country only.

BOWLES, F., ed., *Access to Higher Education*. Paris: UNESCO, 1963.

172  Comparative Studies and Educational Decision

HUSEN, T., ed. *International Study of Achievement in Mathematics.* New York: John Wiley, 1967.
MAJAULT, J. *Primary and Secondary Education: Modern Trends and Common Problems.* Strasbourg: Council of Europe, 1967.
REUCHLIN, M. *Pupil Guidance: Facts and Problems.* Strasbourg: Council of Europe, 1964.

5. EDUCATION AND PLANNING

ANDERSON, C. A., and M. J. BOWMAN, eds. *Education and Economic Development.* London: Frank Cass, 1966.
*Curriculum Improvement and Educational Development.* Paris: O.E.C.D., 1966.
*Elements of Educational Planning.* Paris: UNESCO, 1963.
HALSEY, A. H., et al. *Education, Economy and Society.* Glencoe: Free Press, 1965.
HARBISON, F. H., and C. A. MYERS. *Education, Manpower, and Economic Growth.* New York: McGraw-Hill, 1964.
KING, E. J. *Education and Social Change.* Oxford and New York: Pergamon Press, 1966.
VAIZEY, J. *The Economics of Education.* London: Faber, 1962.

6. SPECIALIZED BIBLIOGRAPHIES

*Analytical Bibliography on Comparative Education.* Paris: UNESCO Division of Comparative Education, 1964.
*Comparative Education Bibliography.* Selected by T. H. BRISTOW and E. H. SCHLICHTER. Hamburg: UNESCO Institute for Education, 1963.
*Economics of Education: A Selected Annotated Bibliography.* Edited by M. BLAUG. Oxford and New York: Pergamon Press, 1966.
*Educational Planning: A Bibliography.* Paris: International Institute for Educational Planning, 1964.
*Teaching Comparative Education: A Bibliographical Guide.* Edited by B. HOLMES and T. H. BRISTOW. Paris: UNESCO, 1964.

7. JOURNALS

*Comparative Education.* Edited by A. D. C. PETERSON, W. D. HALLS, and E. J. KING. Editorial office: Oxford University Department of Education.

*Comparative Education Review.* Edited by H. J. NOAH. Editorial office: Teachers College, Columbia University, New York.

*International Review of Education.* Edited by G. ÖGREN. Editorial office: UNESCO Institute for Education, Hamburg.

*index*

Absolutes, 7
Addams, Jane, 105
Alarm clock, 33
Analysis, 88
Applied sciences, 24, 46, 110
Arab countries, 146
Area of decision, 49, 160ff.
Area studies, 140
Arnold, M., 85
Articulation of problems, 125, 154, 163
Assimilation of ideas, 120
Atomic energy, 46
Attitudes and institutions, 90
"Authorities", 127ff.
Authority, 45, 124, 134, 135, 144
Automation, 63
Autonomy of cultures, 58

Bagrit, Sir L., 63
Barnard, H. C., 85
Barnard, Henry, 85
Beeby, C. E., 120, 149
Benedict, R., 87
Benn, S. I., 6, 52
Bentham, J., 54
Bereday, G. Z. F., 83, 84, 86, 88
Binding consequences, 45
Birth control, 46
Blaug, M., 61
Block interaction, 153
"Borrowing", 84ff.
Bowles, F., 148

Bowman, M. J., 113
"Brain drain", 118, 129
Brameld, T., 105
Bremen plan, 8
Britain, 80
Buddhism, 35
Budgeting, 60
Business and education, 133
Business investments in research, 114

Catholic outlook, 35
Causation, 9, 11, 41, 46, 52, 113
Ceremonial, 10
Certainty, 7, 79
Change, 37, 78, 125, 141
Chicago, University of, 64
China, 147
Christianity, 86, 104
Churches, 37
Civil service, 125
Clarke, Sir F., 105
Climaxes, 47
Colombo Plan, 145
Commissions, 126–127
Communication, 40, 51, 56, 60, 66, 94, 95, 99, 111, 125, 127–128, 130, 157ff.
Communism, 34, 163
Communist education, 89, 164
Comparative attitude, 96, 129, 135

175

Comparative education, 1ff., 47, 64, 81ff., 94, 137ff.; departments of, 124; societies for, 125; as subject-matter, 51, 70, 138
*Comparative Education*, 150
*Comparative Education Review*, 150
Comparative methods, 43ff., 71ff., 110ff.
Comparative studies, 1, 91, 96, 102, 129; changes in, 81ff., 91, 96, 138
Comparison, feasibility of, 32, 41, 43ff., 71ff.
Compatibility, 86
"Computable model", 61
Computers, 51, 64, 66, 67
Conant, J. B., 138
Conceptual framework, 3, 23ff., 47, 89, 94, 111, 135, 138
Conceptual model, 23ff., 52, 112, 123
Concern, 28
Conferences, 100
Constituent awareness, 16
"Constituent conversation", 128, 132
Context, 46, 48, 56ff., 64. See also Climax, Conceptual framework, "Cultural envelope", Dynamics, Ecology, "Logic of situations", Perception, Readiness, Symbolism, "Whole view" of society
Contingency, 51, 52
Continuous decision-making, 132, 134, 136
Control, 35, 75

Co-operative scholarship, **64ff.**, 68, 92, 93, 95, 99, 125, 149, 151
Copying, 84ff.
Corporate authority, 134
Council of Europe, 116, 148
Countries as basis for study, 142
Cramer, J. F., and G. S. Browne, 148
Creativity, 75, 164–165
Cremin, L. A., 85, 91
Cross-cultural comparisons, 47, 67, 98
Crystal Palace, 85
"Cultural envelope", 10, 15
Cultural idioms or patterns, 47, 57–58
Culture, 12, 15, 143

Darwin, C., 54
Data banks, 131
de Gaulle, C., 78
de Witt, N., 148
Decentralised countries, 122, 146
Decision, 2, 40, 46, 48, 69, 92, 96, 103ff., 154
Decision-making institutions, 114, 116, 145
Democracy, 36
Denmark, 144
Department of Education and Science (U.K.), 81, 157
"Description", 53, 89
Detachment, 27, 48
Determinants, 7n, 37
Determinism, 45, 49, 53
Developing countries, 93, 97, 118

Development studies, 65, 90, 101ff.
Developmental considerations, 20, 41, 49, 113ff., 118, 152, 159
Dewey, J., 91, 105, 109, 164
Diez-Hochleitner, R., 115
Diffusion of responsibility, 110
Discussion, arrangements for, 108, 114, 128, 132, 134, 136
Dogmatic Fallacy, 37
Driving forces, 87
Dualism, 75
Dynamics of situations, 32, 49, 50

Ecology, 10, 54, 68, 73
Economic studies, 90
Economics of education, 61, 63
Education, formal, 78–79, 84, 117, 162
"Education industry", 133
Educational planning, 19. See also Planning
"Educative society", 104–105
Eisenstadt, S. N., 90
Electronic devices, 64
Elementary education, 120
Elvin, H. L., 107
*Embourgeoisement*, 33
Empirical studies, 21, 64ff., 89, 95, 106ff., 150
European Economic Community, 68, 122, 132, 145
Examination of conscience, 113, 122
Excellence, 144
"Existential" awareness, 135. See also Involvement

Experience, importance of, 99, 135, 155–156
Experts, 36, 45
"Explosion"
  of commitment, 79
  of population, 79

Factors, 58, 74, 147
Feasibility, 95, 110
Feed-back, 10, 11, 75, 99, 135, 156
Fernig, L., 84
Field theory, 9
Fisher Act, 77
Follow-up action, 100ff.
Forces, 9, 74, 87
Forecasting. See Prediction
Formal education, 78–79, 84, 117, 162
Formulae, 45
France, 146
"Frontier of interaction", 153

Galbraith, J. K., 114
Galsworthy, J., 159
Genetic code or "laws", 54
German bishops, 8
*Gestalt*, 40
Governmental responsibilities, 124, 126, 129, 135–136
Grafting, 86
Great Exhibition, 85
"Great Society", 164
Grenoble, France, 160
Growing points, 44, 75
Guilt, 10

Habits, 55
Halsey, A. H., 113, 120

Hans, N., 82ff., 87, 147
Heresy, 39
Higher education, meaning of, 18
Hindus, 44
Hitler, A., 88
Holmes, B., 53–54
Hughes, H. S., 54
*Humanisme du travail*, 39
Hypothesis, 6n, 8, 9, 25, 44ff., 48, 49, 53, 75, 95, 107

Identification, 17ff., 32, 41, 56, 59
Ideology, 34ff., 41. See also Conceptual framework, Occasion, Perception, "Whole view" of society
Implementing decisions, 96, 111, 126ff. See also Training
Importations, 85–86
Industrial Revolution, 133, 145
Industrial Training Act, 77
Industrialization, 16, 37, 73–74, 95
Infantilism, 4, 37
Information, 97, 108, 113, 121, 124. See also Communication, "Intelligence"
Information services, 127, 130–132
Input and output, 113
Institutionalised scholarship, 65, 95, 101, 111, 151
Institutions: and attitudes, 55, 90, 104–105; for decision, 114, 136
"Intelligence" for decision, 116, 129, 136
Intelligence quotient (I.Q.), 107

Interdependence, 16, 122, 132, 160
International contacts, 111, 125
International education, 91
International Institute of Educational Planning, 65, 115, 119, 145
International Study of Achievement in Mathematics, 47, 64, 151
Involvement, 36, 56, 77, 83–84, 88, 164. See also Context, Culture, Ideology, Perception, "Whole view" of society
Islam, 35
Isolation, 135

Japan, 80, 84, 97, 147
Jefferson, T., 91
Jesuits, 86, 144
Journals, 100
Judaism, 143

Kandel, I. L., 82
Keppel, F., 122, 124, 132
Knowledge, changes in, 78, 105

Langevin-Wallon reforms, 77
"Language of perception", 12. See also Conceptual framework, Culture, Ideology, "Logic of situations", Perception, Symbolism, "Whole view" of society
"Laws", 5–9, 12–15, 49, 53–54
"Leap-frogging", 62
Learning, 11, 44, 79
Levels of interest, 100
Literacy, 160
Literary studies, 140

"Logic of situations", 6, 73, 113, 121
London University Institute of Education, 65
Love, 55

"Making up our minds", 109
Mallinson, V., 83, 143
Malthus, T., 54
"Mandarins", 126
Mann, Horace, 85
Mannheim, K., 34, 104
Marx, K., 54
Marxism, 15, 32–34, 92
Mass production, 33
Meaning of words and ideas, 17, 52, 95
Mechanics' institutes, 73
Medawar, Sir P., 39
Meiji Restoration, 84
Method, 37
Methodology, 24ff., 55, 69
Methods of study, 55, 137ff.
Mill, J. S., 39
Ministers, 126
Ministry of Technology, 114
Models, 32, 52
Monitorial system, 85
Moral code, 55
Moscow, 91
Moser, C. A., 62
Mussolini, B., 88

Naming, 45
Napoleon, 85
"National character", 87, 143
National decisions, 116, 118
National Foundation for Educational Research, 157
National Science Foundation, 67

Nationalism, 87–88
Newsom Report, 156
*Nomos*, 6
Normative example, 55
Norms, 13, 55
Nuffield Foundation, 67

Objectivity, 1ff., 23ff.
Objects, 26
Obsolescence, 108, 122, 132
Occasion, 28, 47
Official statements, 156
Operation Headstart, 156
Operational considerations, 96, 102
Organisation for Economic Co-operation and Development (O.E.C.D.), 90, 145
Orthodoxy, 39
Owen, R., 104, 164

"Pace-setters", 120, 160
"Parliament for educational policy", 125, 129
Partiality, 40, 121
Partnership, 164
Patterns, 11ff., 87. *See also* Conceptual framework, Cultural envelope, "Logic of situations", Perception, "Whole view" of society
Peace Corps, 140
Perception, 11, 26ff., 36, 40, 54, 94
Peters, R. S., 6, 52
Philadelphia Centennial Exhibition, 85
Planning, 40, 81, 115ff., 119, 146
Pluralism, 75

Pluralistic society, 30, 75
Policy-making bodies, 124
Policy studies, 93, 115, 119, 125
Political considerations, 77, 81, 83, 88, 91, 122, 124
Polytechnical education, 39
Popper, Sir K., 6ff., 44, 49ff., 54, 74ff., 113
Precision, 40
Prediction, 8, 49, 52, 62, 65, 75, 87
Primary education, 120
Principles, 8
Priority, 95, 110, 113, 142
Private choice, 35
Probability, 52
Problem-solving, 56, 109
Problem studies, 58ff., 77ff., 98ff., 147ff.
Procedural pattern, 71ff., 81, 102, 110, 129, 141, 152. *See also* Research, Specificity
"Process of decision", 132ff.
Profitability, 61
Programmes, 67
Protestantism, effect of, 134
Public education, 78
Public service, 60
Punctuality, 33
Pure research, 71
Pure science, 46
Purpose, 3, 28, 40, 43ff., 76ff., 83, 86, 153
Pyramids of excellence, 120, 160

Quality, considerations of, 63
Quantitative studies, 24, 40, 51, 63
Questions, procedural, 152. *See also* Problem studies

Readiness, 77, 86, 113, 164
Reconstruction, 88, 91
Reform considerations, 72, 80, 150, 162
Regularities, 15, 73, 75
Reguzzoni, M., 8
Relativity, 141
Relevance, 30, 69
Reliability, 47
Reorientation of education, 126. *See also* Reform considerations
Research, 107, 131, 157ff.; in comparative education, 98ff., 150, 154; design of, 48, 68; methods of, 48, 55ff., 59ff., 72, 75, 93, 152; *see also* Strategy
Research units, 65, 114, 163
"Research and development", 114
*Responsables de demain*, 132
Retrieval systems, 64, 105, 131
Review of institutions and decisions, 108ff., 132
Ricardo, D., 54
Robbins Report, 47, 62, 148
Robinsohn, S. B., 84
Roles, 29, 95
Roman Catholicism, 86, 144
Rumpelstiltskin, 45

Saclay, France, 108
Sadler, Sir M., 86
Sargent, Sir J., 120
Schneider, F., 87, 147
School-leaving age, 159
School, meaning of, 18, 30ff.
School systems, 84, 89, 97
Schools Council, 67

Science: meaning of, 24ff., 38; methods of, 39
"Scientific research workers", 163
Secondary education, 119, 120, 159
Self, consciousness of, 141
Self-determination, 144
Self-sufficiency, 118
Sense of direction, 90, 141, 142, 153
Service occupations, 81
Shils, E., 57ff., 89
Significance, 12, 61
Singule, F., 92
Snow, Lord, 126
Social aspects of decision, 46
Social categories in education, 72
Social change, 73
Social demand, 62
Social engineering, 25
Social influences on intelligence, 107
Social sciences, 21, 24
"Sociological laws", 6, 14, 52–54
Sociology, 13ff., 57ff., 140
Soviet Union, 39, 80, 97, 146. See also Marxism
Special language, 56, 69
Specialisation, effect of, 134
Specificity of research, 56, 59, 72, 75, 93
Speculative treatment, 21
Statics, 50
Strategy in comparative education, 71ff., 81, 102, 110, 129
Strategy of decision, 106, 110, 116, 124, 158
Subjects, 26

Superstitions, 159
Sussex, University of, 65
Sweden, 97
Symbolism, 11ff., 14, 39, 86. See also Conceptual framework, Cultural envelope, "Logic of situations", Perception, "Whole view" of society

Tactics, 129
Teacher education, 3, 66, 82, 88, 101, 110, 118, 119, 138ff.
Teacher's role, 161
Team research. See Co-operative scholarship
Technical aid, 92
Technology, influence of, 15, 52, 73
Telecommunications, 125
Term papers, 155
Theory, 69. See also Hypothesis
Time-scale, 126
Totalitarian states, 36
Toulouse, France, 160
Tsang, C.-S., 147
Trade unions, 37
Training, 96, 101, 132
Transcendence, 17, 47, 74
Trends, 6, 24, 49
Trial-and-error methods, 74

Uncertainty, 11, 44, 79
Understanding, 36
Undressing children, 5
UNESCO, 65, 84, 116ff.
University organisations, 66ff., 130
Urbanisation, 16, 74
United States, 80, 97, 118, 134

United States Office of Education, 146, 157
Union of Soviet Socialist Republics, 38, 80, 97, 146

Verification, 94
Viet Nam, 52
Votes, 113

"Waves", 74
Weber, M., 74
Weizsäcker, C. von, 134

West Germany, 134
Whitehead, A. N., 24, 27
"Whole view" of society or occasion, 30, 36, 40, 41, 46, 47, 49, 51, 57, 75, 77, 87, 89, 94, 105, 107, 113, 115, 117
Wholeness of cultural dynamic, 11–13, 20, 35, 47, 57ff., 75, 89, 117
Wisconsin, University of, 65
World Year Book of Education, 149

For Product Safety Concerns and Information please contact our EU
representative GPSR@taylorandfrancis.com
Taylor & Francis Verlag GmbH, Kaufingerstraße 24, 80331 München, Germany

www.ingramcontent.com/pod-product-compliance
Lightning Source LLC
Chambersburg PA
CBHW051645230426
43669CB00013B/2442